The Shadow Banker's Secrets

Investment Banking for Alternatives

Benjamin D. Summers

Copyright © 2020 Benjamin D. Summers

ALL RIGHTS RESERVED. This book contains material protected under International and Federal Copyright Laws and Treaties. Any unauthorized reprint or use of this material is prohibited. No part of this book may be reproduced or transmitted in any form or by any means, electronic or mechanical, including photocopying, recording, or by any information storage and retrieval system, without express written permission from the author/publisher.

ISBN 978-1-64184-131-3 (Hardcover)

ISBN 978-1-64184-132-0 (Paperback)

ISBN 978-1-64184-133-7 (Ebook)

LCCN: 2019956965

Published by Adagio Institute, Inc., Houston, Texas.

TABLE OF CONTENTS

Disclosures & Disclaimers vii

Introduction ix

Prologue: Deciphering Monetary Policy 1
   The Federal Reserve and Systemically Important Banks . . . 2
   Benefits from the Fed 11
   O Canada, A Successful Alternative to Central
   Banking 16
   Effects of U.S. Monetary Policy on the Greater
   Economy 18
   Moving Against the Market Movers 28

Preface 31
   The Golden Rule: Whoever ~~Has the Gold~~
   Understands Money Makes the Rules 31
   What is a Shadow Bank? 32
   Who Is This For? 33
   Syndicators vs. Financial Institutions 34
   Your Goals & My Objective 36
   Ben Summers & Adagio Group 42

TABLE OF CONTENTS

Secret #1: Engineering Risk-Adjusted Investment Performance 59
    What is Risk? 59
    Smart vs. Dumb Money: Odd Lot Theory 63
    Financial Crises 65
    An Introduction to Risk Analysis in Numbers— the Coin Flip 67
    The Case of the Two and a Half Billion Percent Return 68
    The Soldier's Bad Bet and Tail Risk 69
    Socialization of Risk: The Federal Reserve 71
    Risk-Adjusted Performance Measures 73
    Summers Alternative Risk Rating 75
    Trend Identification 80
    Residential Real Estate Fundamentals 81
    Derivatives—Control the Risk-Adjusted Returns of Any Asset 85
    Quantitative Risk Management Applied to Real Estate 91
    Benefits of Quantitative Risk Analysis 94
    Secret #1 Summary 99

Secret #2: Creating Capital 101
    Private Securities Issuance & The Savings Crisis 101
    Capital Structure 104
    Capital Markets 106
    Traditional Portfolios 109

TABLE OF CONTENTS

    Private Investment Companies........................ 111

    Delaware Statutory Trusts 119

    Creating & Selling Private Securities Basics 121

    Raising Money – The Tale of Two Typical Client Profiles 123

    Secret #2 Summary 127

Secret #3: Navigating Regulatory Compliance 129

    Introduction to Securities Law....................... 129

    The Woodbridge Case Study 130

    A Few Securities Law Considerations Commonly Ignored by Unlicensed Issuers 132

    Broker-Dealer, RIA & Family Office Esoteric Considerations 133

    The Investment Club—An Underutilized Feeder Structure... 134

    Secret #3 Summary 137

Applying the Three Secrets & Tailored Solutions 139

    Buy Side vs. Sell Side—A Role for Everyone.......... 139

    Financial Advisors 142

    Other Financial Professionals....................... 145

    Retail and Institutional Investors 146

    Alternative Asset Managers/Sponsors 147

    The Shadow Banker's Secrets Program 149

Epilogue: The Three Economic Roles 181

TABLE OF CONTENTS

Appendix: Questions and Answers 185
  How to Take Advantage of our Debt-Backed Currency. 185
  What Would Result from an Asset-Backed Currency. 187
  What Will the Next Crisis Look Like 190
  How to Protect Yourself from Economic Collapse. 193
  DIY Real Estate. 196
  Alternatives to Real Estate 198
  Backtested Risk-Adjusted Performance for Private Equity. 201
  How to Use Debt 204
  How to Use Personal Debt. 206
  How to Take Advantage of Inflation. 211
  What to Do as an Employee 213
  How to Calculate Risk. 215
  Risk in Words and Numbers 217
  Using Risk Measures 219
  Investment Club Issues 220
  What Investment Banks Do. 222
  What Financial Advisors Need to Know. 223
  The Purpose of This Book 225
  Creating Monetizable Value. 227

About The Author. 229

Disclosures & Disclaimers

THE INFORMATION AND MATERIALS HEREIN ARE PROVIDED ONLY FOR GENERAL BUSINESS GUIDANCE. THE APPLICATION AND IMPACT OF THIS INFORMATION CAN VARY WIDELY BASED ON SPECIFIC FACTS INVOLVED. FURTHERMORE, GIVEN THE CHANGING NATURE OF LAWS, RULES, AND REGULATIONS, THERE CAN BE NO ASSURANCE THAT THE DESCRIPTIONS AND INFORMATION IN THIS BOOK WILL REMAIN ACCURATE OR APPROPRIATE. ACCORDINGLY, THE INFORMATION AND MATERIALS IN THIS BOOK ARE PROVIDED TO YOU WITH YOUR EXPRESS UNDERSTANDING AND AGREEMENT THAT THE AUTHORS AND PUBLISHERS ARE NOT ENGAGED IN RENDERING (AND YOU ARE NOT RELYING ON THIS PRESENTATION FOR ANY) LEGAL, FINANCIAL, TAX, OR ANY OTHER PROFESSIONAL ADVICE OR SERVICES. YOU ARE STRONGLY ENCOURAGED TO CONSULT WITH YOUR OWN COMPETENT FINANCE, TAX, LEGAL, OR OTHER PROFESSIONAL ADVISOR.

NEITHER THIS BOOK NOR ANY OF ITS CONTENTS SHALL CONSTITUTE AN OFFER TO SELL OR THE SOLICITATION OF AN OFFER TO BUY INTERESTS IN ANY FUND OR ENTITY. ANY DOCUMENTS SUCH AS SUMMARIES, FACT CARDS, PRESENTATIONS, PRIVATE PLACEMENT MEMORANDA, SUBSCRIPTION AGREEMENTS, OPERATING AGREEMENTS, ETC. INCLUDED IN THIS BOOK ARE FOR INFORMATIONAL PURPOSES ONLY.

THE MATERIALS INCLUDED WITH THIS PRESENTATION ARE PROVIDED SOLELY FOR INFORMATIONAL PURPOSES AND ARE NOT TO BE REPRODUCED OR DISTRIBUTED.

Introduction

Welcome, and thank you for reading this book on how you, as a financial market participant—from retail investor to asset manager or financial advisor—can beat the market, protect yourself from financial crises, and if you so choose, scale your investment business or portfolio to nine figures and beyond, even if you don't have an existing track record.

I know many of you are well aware of the dysfunction and even corruption of the banking and financial services industry:

- How the Fed, which is effectively run by the banking cartel, creates and controls the entire money supply of the U.S.,
- How well-intentioned financial advisors are prisoners of overreaching regulation,
- How unwitting asset managers continually fall victim to invisible legal traps as they try to raise money, and
- How all of this leads to retail investors being stuck with limited investment options that all seem doomed to fail with the next inevitable crash.

When I talk to people about this subject, the typical response I get is, "Great, but what could I possibly do about it?" This book will lay out exactly what you can do.

INTRODUCTION

We're going to walk (if not jog) through the process of how you can create highly valuable capital out of thin air almost exactly the same way the Federal Reserve and banking system creates the modern U.S. dollar. We're going to reveal the Shadow Banker's Secrets.

Prologue
Deciphering Monetary Policy

Monetary policy and its effect on the markets can often seem like an impossibly complex, if not opaque, dynamic. The market obviously responds, and most often in a seemingly positive manner, to the actions taken by the Federal Reserve System and statements by its chairman, but how, why, and what are the less obvious effects of a centralized monetary system?

Money is a market-chosen commodity that serves as a recognizable, divisible, and portable medium of exchange and store of value. Historically, gold and silver have served this function. The term "dollar" as cited in the U.S. Constitution (Article 1, Section 9, Clause 1 and the 7th Amendment) and specifically defined under the Coinage Act of 1792 *"to contain three hundred and seventy-one grains and four sixteenth parts of a grain of pure, or four hundred and sixteen grains of standard silver"* is a reference to the Spanish milled dollar, a silver coin. The authors of the U.S. Constitution had learned the dangers of issuing unchecked fiat currency first-hand when the Continental Congress issued its own paper currency, the infamous Continental, as allowed under the Articles of Confederation. The result was economic chaos. In one of the only instances in world history where the politicians who created an egregious problem recognized their mistake and corrected it, the Continental Congress later repaired to Philadelphia, drafting the U.S. Constitution explicitly maintaining gold and silver as tender in payment of debts (Article 1, Section 10, Clause 1). Centuries of pressures to fund war and appease the banking cartel have ultimately reversed this act of wisdom.[1]

THE FEDERAL RESERVE AND SYSTEMICALLY IMPORTANT BANKS

The Federal Reserve System ("the Fed") is the central banking system of the United States. The Fed is said to be independent within the government in that *"its monetary policy decisions do not have to be approved by the president or anyone else in the executive or legislative branches of government."* The Fed has both private and public aspects. There are twelve Federal Reserve Banks that are owned by their respective member banks while the Board of Governors, which is a federal agency in and of itself, is appointed by the president of the United States.[2] It is worth noting that other than the 6% dividend paid to the Fed's shareholders (i.e., its member banks), the profits of the Fed are returned to the U.S. Treasury, and member banks do not exercise the proprietary control traditionally associated with the concept of ownership beyond the statutory dividend.[3] Member banks do, however, elect six of the nine directors for their regional Federal Reserve Bank board, and each Federal Reserve Bank board of directors appoints its bank president. Ownership in the twelve Federal Reserve Banks is not public record, but national banks must be

---

1. Edwin Vieira Jr., *Pieces of Eight: The Monetary Powers and Disabilities of the United States Constitution* (2nd ed.), Sheridan Books, 2002
2. "FAQ - Who owns the Federal Reserve?" Board of Governors of the Federal Reserve System. Retrieved September 14, 2012. (http://www.federalreserve.gov/faqs/about_14986.htm)
3. Michael D. Reagan, "The Political Structure of the Federal Reserve System," *American Political Science Review*, Vol. 55 (March 1961), pp. 64-76, as reprinted in Money and Banking: Theory, Analysis, and Policy, p. 153, ed. by S. Mittra (Random House, New York 1970).

members while state-chartered banks may become members by meeting certain requirements.

The Fed was established via the Federal Reserve Act, which was passed by Congress and signed into law by President Woodrow Wilson on December 23, 1913. The passage of this act granted the Fed exclusive right to issue the U.S. national currency, Federal Reserve Notes, at the discretion of its Board of Governors with the five regional Fed Bank presidents making up the Federal Open Market Committee ("FOMC"). Federal Reserve Notes, or "dollars," were redeemable in gold until the Emergency Banking Act of 1933 removed that obligation. Federal Reserve Notes from that point on were redeemable only for other Federal Reserve Notes (effectively making change). On April 5, 1933, President Franklin Roosevelt signed Executive Order 6102 criminalizing the possession of monetary gold in quantities exceeding $100. All U.S. citizens and businesses were required to deliver their gold to the Fed in exchange for $20.67 per once. The price of gold was then raised by the Treasury to $35 per ounce. Although citizens could not possess gold, the federal government continued to maintain a stable international gold price until 1968 when it rose to $42.22 before the gold window was closed altogether under President Richard Nixon in 1971. This move led to The Great Inflation of the 1970s. The limitation on private ownership of gold in the U.S. was repealed in 1974 under President Gerald Ford. In 1977, Congress amended the Federal Reserve Act, stating the monetary policy objectives of the Federal Reserve, its "dual mandate," as:

> *"The Board of Governors of the Federal Reserve System and the Federal Open Market Committee shall maintain long run growth of the monetary and credit aggregates commensurate with the economy's long run potential to increase production, so as to promote effectively the goals of maximum employment, stable prices and moderate long-term interest rates."*

By January 1980, gold had risen to $850 per ounce. Under Fed Chairman Paul Volcker, the FOMC raised the federal funds rate, which is the interest rate banks charge each other for loans from their reserve balances with the Fed, to 20% in June 1980, successfully stabilizing the dollar.

How does the Fed accomplish its "dual mandate?" The Fed has several tools at its disposal to set interest rates and ultimately control the money supply. They include establishing reserve requirements, setting the target federal funds rate (which includes the use of reverse repos and paying interest on reserves), adjusting the discount rate (which is what banks pay to borrow directly from the Fed in an emergency), and open market operations ("OMO"). The most commonly used tool of the Fed is open market operations. Two examples of OMO are quantitative easing ("QE") and Operation Twist. In the last rendition of Operation Twist (2011–2012), the Fed affected the yield curve of U.S. Treasury securities by simultaneously selling short-term debt and buying long-term debt via the ostensibly private market of primary dealers. (The Fed's balance sheet remained unchanged.)[4] The result maintained artificially low interest rates on long-term U.S. debt, which subsequently brought down the overall market interest for long-term debt. QE is the process by which the Fed increases its own balance sheet by creating Federal Reserve Notes (U.S. dollars) to buy financial assets (e.g., U.S. Treasuries and mortgage-backed securities, "MBS") from the market, thereby increasing the monetary base. (This process is often referred to as "printing money," although technically speaking, the act of physical printing is conducted by the Bureau of Engraving and Printing, a government agency within the United States Department of the Treasury.)

---

4. "Maturity Extension Program and Reinvestment Policy". Board of Governors of the Federal Reserve System. Retrieved September 28, 2012. (http://www.federalreserve.gov/monetarypolicy/maturityextensionprogram.htm)

S&P 500 Index performance from April 2008 to
October 2012 highlighting the influence of Fed intervention.

In fact, this is the primary mechanism by which money is created: the Fed creates U.S. dollars at its own discretion to buy primarily interest-bearing U.S. Treasury securities, or Treasuries (e.g., T-bills, T-Notes, T-Bonds, and TIPS), which, of course, increases the federal debt. In other words, since closing the gold window in 1971, Federal Reserve Notes are effectively backed by nothing more than the government's promise to pay Federal Reserve Notes. As should be obvious, the result is a circular process in which the U.S. currency has a value supported solely by perception. This perceived value is quite strong, however, as the U.S. dollar remains entrenched as the de facto reserve currency of the world as established by the now-extinct Bretton Woods Agreement of 1944 when the dollar was pegged to gold at $35 per ounce.

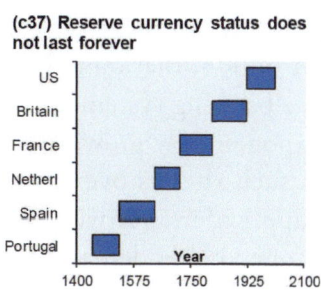

Historical world reserve currencies from 1400 to present.

PROLOGUE: DECIPHERING MONETARY POLICY

US Monetary Base (adjusted for Changes in Reserve Requirements)
January 1, 1970 to November 30, 2009

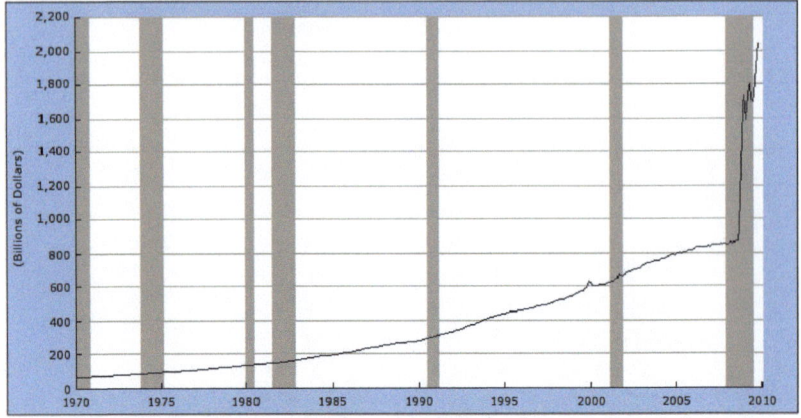

Source: St Louis Federal Reserve, database: FRED® (Federal Reserve Economic Data)

The Adjusted Monetary Base is the sum of currency (including coin) in circulation outside Federal Reserve Banks and the U.S. Treasury, plus deposits held by depository institutions at Federal Reserve Banks. These data are adjusted for the effects of changes in statutory reserve requirements on the quantity of base money held by depositories.

The monetary base created by the Fed is then multiplied by the process of fractional reserve banking, which is also predicated on increasing debt. Currently, the Fed's reserve requirement for depository institutions with over $124.2 million in net transaction accounts (i.e., demand deposit accounts) is 10%. This means that if a bank is capitalized at $100 million, either from deposits or otherwise, it can lend out ten times that amount, or $1 billion; that money then becomes additional deposits within the banking system allowing the process to repeat ad infinitum, exponentially growing the money supply. The result, by design, is such that as overall debt increases or decreases, so does the supply of money with the only real constraint on banks creating money being demand for loans. In other words, instead of the money supply being tied to the total value of goods and services in the economy, it's tied to the total amount of bank-issued debt.

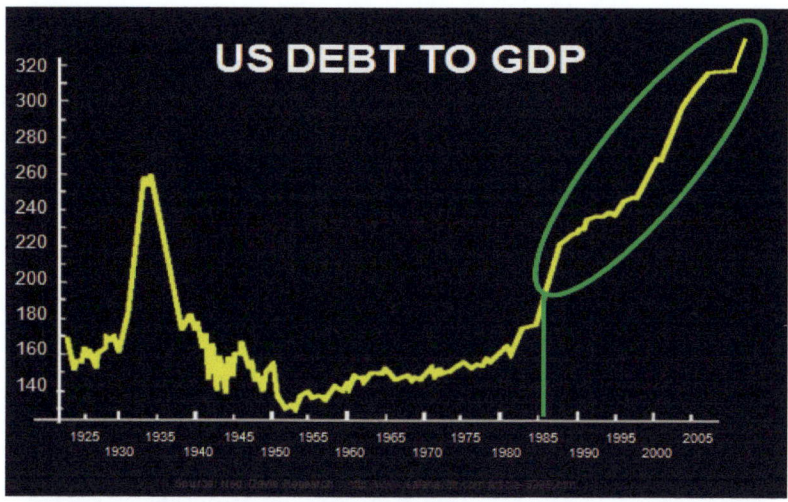

U.S. Total Credit Market Debt to GDP ratio from 1922 to 2010. Total Credit Market Debt is the total outstanding debt owed by all sectors (households, corporations, farms, state and local governments, federal government, financial companies, and foreigners) and includes open market paper, Treasuries, agencies, municipal bonds, corporate and foreign bonds, bank loans, other loans and advances, mortgages, and consumer credit.

Fractional reserve banking is inherently unstable. If it weren't, there would be no need for a "lender of last resort:"

> *Any exponential, debt-based monetary system is, at its very core, a Ponzi scheme. It simply has to keep expanding so that there's enough money and credit manufactured today to meet yesterday's principal and interest loads. Without endless growth, sooner or later the debt pile collapses, and truly extraordinary losses are taken by somebody.*[5]

With the financial crisis of 2008 and under the pretense of "too big to fail," Congress passed the Emergency Economic Stabilization Act establishing the Troubled Asset Relief Program ("TARP"), which authorized the U.S. Treasury to spend up to

---

5. Chris Martenson, "What to Do When Every Market Is Manipulated," *Peak Prosperity*, August 15, 2012, http://www.peakprosperity.com/blog/79470/what-dowhen-every-market-manipulated (accessed September 21, 2012)

$700 billion buying distressed assets and supplying cash directly to banks, in addition to allowing the Fed to make interest payments on depository institutions' required and excess reserve balances. Meanwhile, the Fed disseminated over $16 trillion[6] in loans and new currency via QE1 and QE2 over the next two years. The Levy Institute estimated that the Fed committed over $29 trillion, increasing its balance sheet from $900 billion to $2.8 trillion.[7] The following table itemizes the recipients of the Fed's bailout allocations according to the GAO:

Table 8: Institutions with Largest Total Transaction Amounts (Not Term-Adjusted) across Broad-Based Emergency Programs (Borrowing Aggregated by Parent Company and Includes Sponsored ABCP Conduits), December 1, 2007 through July 21, 2010

Dollar in billions

Borrowing Parent Company	TAF	PDCF	TSLF	CPFF	Subtotal	AMLF	TALF	Total loans
Citigroup Inc.	$110	$2,020	$348	$33	$2,511	$1	-	$2,513
Morgan Stanley	-	1,913	115	4	2,032	-	9	2,041
Merrill Lynch & Co.	0	1,775	166	8	1,949	-	-	1,949
Bank of America Corporation	280	947	101	15	1,342	2	-	1,344
Barclays PLC (United Kingdom)	232	410	187	39	868	-	-	868
Bear Stearns Companies, Inc.	-	851	2	-	853	-	-	853
Goldman Sachs Group Inc.	-	589	225	0	814	-	-	814
Royal Bank of Scotland Group PLC (United Kingdom)	212	-	291	39	541	-	-	541
Deutsche Bank AG (Germany)	77	1	277	-	354	-	-	354
UBS AG (Switzerland)	56	35	122	75	287	-	-	287
JP Morgan Chase & Co.	99	112	68	-	279	111	-	391
Credit Suisse Group AG (Switzerland)	0	2	261	-	262	0	-	262
Lehman Brothers Holdings Inc.	-	83	99	-	183	-	-	183
Bank of Scotland PLC (United Kingdom)	181	-	-	-	181	-	-	181
BNP Paribas SA (France)	64	66	41	3	175	-	-	175
Wells Fargo & Co.	159	-	-	-	159	-	-	159
Dexia SA (Belgium)	105	-	-	53	159	-	-	159
Wachovia Corporation	142	-	-	-	142	-	-	142
Dresdner Bank AG (Germany)	123	0	1	10	135	-	-	135
Societe Generale SA (France)	124	-	-	-	124	-	-	124
All other borrowers	1,854	146	14	460	2,475	103	62	2,639
Total	$3,818	$8,951	$2,319	$738	$15,826	$217	$71	$16,115

Source: GAO analysis of Federal Reserve System data.

This table from the U.S. Government Accountability Office 2011 report "Federal Reserve System: Opportunities Exist to Strengthen Policies and Processes for Managing Emergency Assistance" lists the recipients of emergency loans and the amounts associated with each government program.

---

6. United States Government Accountability Office, Federal Reserve System: Opportunities Exist to Strengthen Policies and Processes for Managing Emergency Assistance. GAO-11-696. (Washington DC: U.S. Government Accountability Office, 2011) www.gao.gov/assets/330/321506.pdf
7. James Felkerson, $29,000,000,000,000: A Detailed Look at the Fed's Bailout by Funding Facility and Recipient. Working Paper No. 698. (Levy Economics Institute of Bard College, 2011) www.levyinstitute.org/pubs/wp_698.pdf

In November 2011, the Financial Stability Board formalized the notion that was popularized by U.S. Congressman Stewart McKinney in a 1984, "too big to fail," publishing a list of global "Systemically Important Financial Institutions", or SIFIs, including 29 banks in 12 countries:

Belgium	China	France	Germany
Dexia	*Bank of China*	*Banque Populaire*	*Commerzbank*
		BNP Paribas	*Deutsche Bank*
		Crédit Agricole	
		Société Générale	

Italy	Japan	Netherlands	Spain
Unicredit	*Mitsubishi Mizuho*	*ING*	*Santander*
	Mizuho FG		
	Sumitomo Mitsui		

Sweden	Switzerland	UK	US
Nordea	*Credit Suisse*	*Barclays*	*Bank of America*
	UBS	*HSBC*	*Bank of New York Mellon*
		Lloyds	*Citigroup*
		Royal Bank of Scotland	*Goldman Sachs*
			JP Morgan
			Morgan Stanley
			State Street
			Wells Fargo

In response to the lack of improvement in unemployment resulting from QE1, QE2, and ongoing Operation Twist, on September 13, 2012, Fed Chairman Ben Bernanke announced the commencement of QE3, launching an open-ended, $40 billion per month, MBS bond-purchasing program. Bernanke stated that QE3 would continue for a considerable time even after unemployment improves, which led to QE3's alternative nickname of QEternity. When asked how buying agency debt would increase employment on proverbial "Main Street," Bernanke responded:

"We are trying to create more employment, we are trying to meet our maximum employment mandate, so that's the objective. Our tools involve—I mean, the tools we have involve affecting financial asset prices, and that's—those are the tools of monetary policy. There are a number of different channels—mortgage rates, I mentioned other interest rates, corporate bond rates, but also the prices of various assets, like, for example, the prices of homes. To the extent that home prices begin to rise, consumers will feel wealthier, they'll feel more disposed to spend. If house prices are rising, people may be more willing to buy homes because they think that they'll, you know, make a better return on that purchase. So house prices is one vehicle. Stock prices—many people own stocks directly or indirectly. The issue here is whether or not improving asset prices generally will make people more willing to spend. One of the main concerns that firms have is there is not enough demand, there's not enough people coming and demanding their products. And if people feel that their financial situation is better because their 401(k) looks better or for whatever reason, their house is worth more, they are more willing to go out and spend, and that's going to provide the demand that firms need in order to be willing to hire and to invest."

The Fed wound down QE3 by October 2014, as the world's central banks picked up the slack with a de facto global QE that has continued to prop up the world's economic house of cards. While the inflation expected from such aggressive monetary policy appears missing from the CPI, it is omnipresent in asset prices across all classes. Fed-induced negative real yields across the fixed-income spectrum have forced conservative savers into risk assets, which has continued to push equities higher. We're now teetering between two tectonic forces: extraordinary inflationary pressures on one side clashed against weak economic fundamentals led by a diminishing middle class on the other. The $13.5-trillion-increase in GDP growth since 2009 has required $17 trillion in additional national debt to achieve.

As of Q3 2018, the Fed reported itself insolvent on a mark-to-market basis in its quarterly financial statements[8]… it is out of dry powder.

BENEFITS FROM THE FED[9, 10, 11]

The primary benefit to the Fed's member banks is not direct profit-sharing in the Fed or interest on reserves but direct access to its low to zero-interest money in addition to the "unintended consequences" of its policies such as inflated asset prices and bank consolidations, which coincidentally have tended to favor its biggest shareholders.

"Free money" loans create moral hazard, which means that those who can borrow money for almost nothing and never have to pay it back act entirely differently from those paying market rates for money and backing their loan with real collateral that is at risk. The SIFI banks are simply not incentivized to participate in the real economy in a productive manner. Why would they, they've got a centrally managed market of Fed-supported returns and risk protection à la the Bernanke-Yellen-Powell Put.

---

8. "Federal Reserve Banks Combined Quarterly Financial Report, Unaudited September 30, 2018". Board of Governors of the Federal Reserve System. Retrieved December 14, 2018. https://www.federalreserve.gov/aboutthefed/files/quarterly-report-20180930.pdf
9. Much of the content in this section is comprised of material taken directly from the sources cited in footnotes 10 and 11. Quotation marks and indentations were not used to minimize excessive, distractive formatting.
10. Charles Hugh Smith, "Cui Bono Fed: Who Benefits from the Federal Reserve?" *Of Two Minds*, September 12, 2012, www.oftwominds.com/blogsept12/cui-bono-Fed9-12.html (accessed September 23, 2012)
11. Chris Martenson, "The Trouble With Printing Money?" *Goldworth Financial*, September 18, 2012, www.goldworth.com/artilcedetail.php?id=364 (accessed September 21, 2012)

PROLOGUE: DECIPHERING MONETARY POLICY

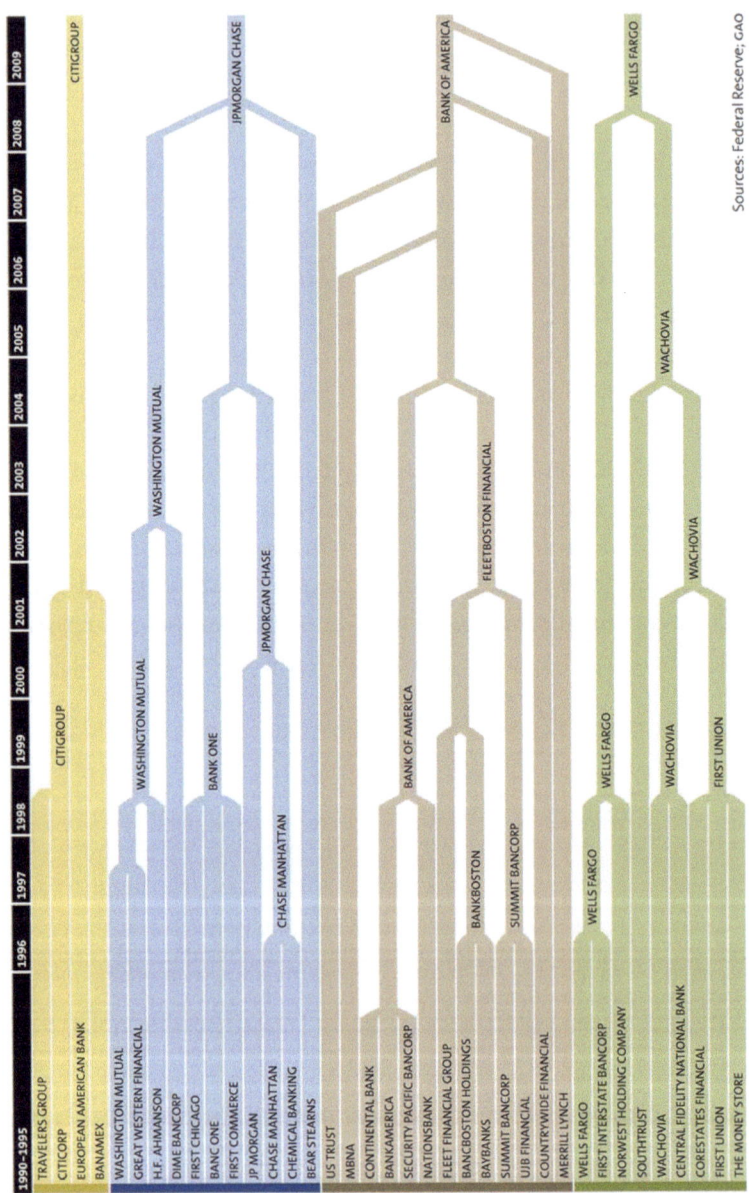

This chart illustrates major financial institution mergers and acquisitions from 1990 through 2009.

In fact, the banking sector's solvency is entirely dependent upon officially sanctioned over-valuation of phantom assets. How does one keep phantom assets inflated? Allow banks to mark assets to fantasy rather than market, keep interest rates at zero to encourage marginally qualified borrowers to take on more debt than is prudent, turning the borrowers into debt-serfs, and buy dodgy debt (such as impaired mortgages) from the banks to clear the bad debt from their books. And, of course, the one thing that can never be done is lending money directly to citizens or buying *their* dodgy mortgages. That wouldn't serve the banks, but QE and Operation Twist do.

QE does this in two ways. First, by dumping money into the banking system, which then has to go somewhere and do something, so some of it ends up in the stock market, and second, by driving down interest rates, which reduces the yield on low-risk assets such as U.S. Treasuries and Certificates of Deposit (CDs) having the tendency to push money into stocks. Why has the Fed been slow to raise rates (2.5% is extraordinarily low by historical standards[12])? As QE3 ended, the rest of the world picked up the stimulus slack. The Fed's slow rate hikes from Q4 2015 through Q4 2018 eventually sent the markets tumbling. The Fed knows that if confidence in the markets falters, it has no more ammunition to reinflate the bubble; hence, rate hikes have ceased. It would seem that the Fed is now trapped such that if it ever pulls away from the market, there will be a rout of historic proportions.

---

12. "Effective Federal Funds Rate 1955 – Present" Federal Economic Data, Federal Reserve Bank of St. Louis Economic Research. Retrieved May 16, 2019. https://fred.stlouisfed.org/series/FEDFUNDS

PROLOGUE: DECIPHERING MONETARY POLICY

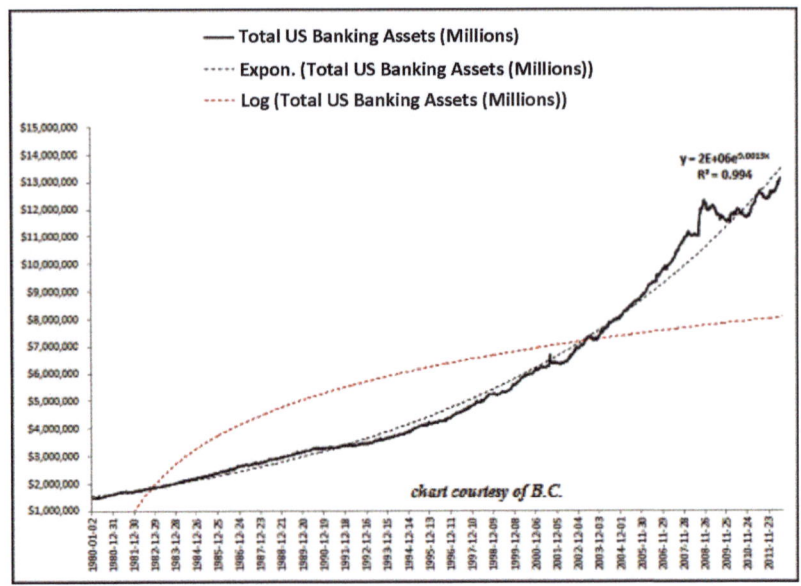

This graph illustrates the growth of U.S. banking assets from 1980 to 2011.

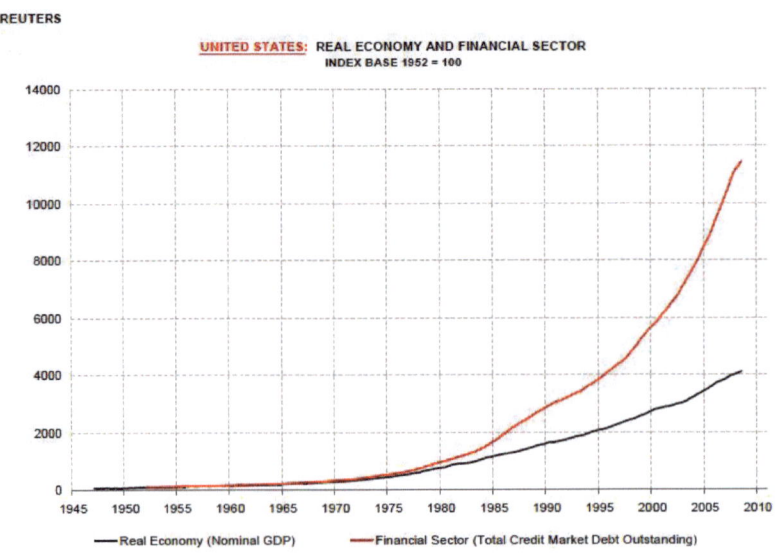

This graph compares the growth of nominal U.S. GDP (not adjusted for inflation) with the growth of the financial sector as measured by total credit market debt outstanding from 1952 to 2009.

Widely distributed prosperity for the citizenry results from increases in real income that flow from productive investments and higher productivity that are passed on to workers. The Fed's model of "prosperity" is to enrich the banks and incentivize workers to take on more debt to boost their consumption of phantom assets in stock and housing bubbles while continuing to inflate the student loan bubble. For example, banks borrow from the Fed at 0%; students borrow from the banks at 7%. Banks never have to actually pay back their "free money" from the Fed, while students are indentured for life to the banks. The interest on skyrocketing debt drains income and capital from potentially productive investments to pay for unproductive debt-based spending on consumption, friction, and mal-investments.

What is the fundamental basis of bank wealth and power? The financialization of the entire economy. And what are the primary mechanisms of financialization? Ever-expanding credit (debt) and leverage based on phantom collateral in phantom assets. And what is the primary purpose of the Fed's policies? To expand debt and leverage. These are the essential mechanisms of increasing the banking sector's wealth, power, and control over the economy and the machinery of governance. Expanding debt and leverage is tantamount to expanding banking profits, and thus, the banks' political power.

The big banks haven't been the only beneficiaries of Fed accommodations, however. Many private funds and foreign companies having questionable economic importance have received funding as well. The following excerpt from a Rolling Stone article, "The Real Housewives of Wall Street," published April 12, 2011, highlights one such example:

> *"...all you have to do is look closely at the taxpayer money handed over to a single company that goes by a seemingly innocuous name: Waterfall TALF Opportunity. At first glance, Waterfall's haul doesn't seem all that huge—just nine loans totaling some $220 million, made through a Fed bailout program. That doesn't seem like a whole lot, considering that Goldman Sachs alone*

received roughly $800 billion in loans from the Fed. But upon closer inspection, Waterfall TALF Opportunity boasts a couple of interesting names among its chief investors: Christy Mack and Susan Karches.

Christy is the wife of John Mack, the chairman of Morgan Stanley. Susan is the widow of Peter Karches, a close friend of the Macks who served as president of Morgan Stanley's investment-banking division. Neither woman appears to have any serious history in business, apart from a few philanthropic experiences. Yet the Federal Reserve handed them both low-interest loans of nearly a quarter of a billion dollars through a complicated bailout program that virtually guaranteed them millions in risk-free income..."

Any healthy political and financial system would have broken this fraud-based system and dismantled the failed banks en masse in an orderly fashion, potentially going so far as to move from a debt-based currency to an asset-backed one. One institution stopped this from happening: the Federal Reserve. Instead of allowing a failed system to collapse and establish a new one based on prudent lending, market-set interest rates, competitive banks, and transparent regulatory structure, the U.S. has a failed system that has become even more politically powerful even as its Fed-backed excesses have increased systemic fragility. In short, the Fed exists to serve the banks and their cronies. Everything else is propaganda.

O CANADA, A SUCCESSFUL ALTERNATIVE TO CENTRAL BANKING

In lieu of fiat currency issued by a central bank, many people advocate for a return to a precious metal standard for currency. While this is likely a better alternative to the debt-based currency system that is currently employed, there are other monetary systems to consider. Canadian history offers a practical example of a successful, elastic alternative to central bank-issued debt-based currency. Until the creation of the Bank of Canada in 1935, Canada utilized an asset-backed currency whose stock varied with demand, unlike its U.S. counterpart where, because of dated Civil War legislation (i.e., National Banking Acts of 1863 and 1864) requiring U.S. National Banks to back currency issuance by U.S. Treasury securities, there was little correlation between economic demand for currency and currency issuance. Competing Canadian banks, on the other hand, were allowed to issue currency backed by general bank assets, the same assets used to back deposits. The following chart compares the stock of U.S. currency to that of Canada during the late 19th century, a period of rapid economic growth characterized by seasonal harvest periods that required increases in currency supply:

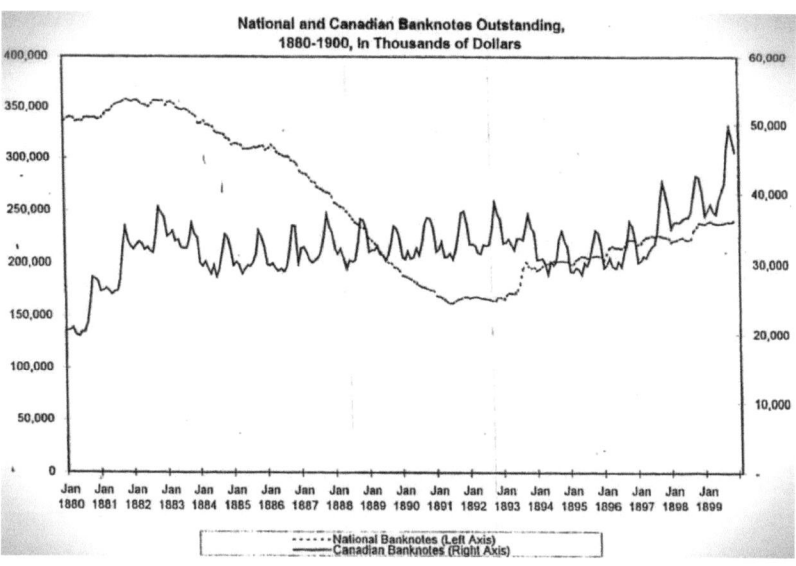

(U.S.) National versus Canadian Banknotes outstanding from 1880 to 1900.

During the Great Depression, Canada did not suffer a single bank failure; the U.S. lost approximately one-third of its banks during that same period. (Canada did lose one bank, Home Bank of Canada, in 1923.) Canada's minimally regulated asset-backed currency system was utilized until populist pro-inflation pressures spearheaded by Major C. H. Douglas led to the creation of Canada's central bank mirroring the U.S. monetary system.[13]

EFFECTS OF U.S. MONETARY POLICY ON THE GREATER ECONOMY[14, 15]

The whole idea of an economy is to allocate land, labor, and capital in a way to maximize productivity and utility of these resources—to increase the standard of living. Capital improves consumers' productivity, and capital is made available through savings. Like any other price, interest rates represent a price to borrow the economy's store of savings and are driven by its supply and demand. When there is a lot of savings, then interest rates, or the costs of money, go down. When there are fewer savings, then interest rates go up. Ultimately, equilibrium will be achieved, creating a market rate of interest.

Money must serve as a store of value to facilitate savings. It's these savings that finance capital investment and business expansion. This investment enables consumers to generate the productivity required to yield the value to purchase goods and services from others. If consumers weren't productive, there would be nothing to buy.

Savings also help drive down prices as they are used to increase production in lieu of immediate consumption; lower prices are a benefit of free markets. The Keynesian argument is that if prices fall, nobody will buy anything as they wait for prices to fall further. The fallacy of this argument is evidenced in the technology sector by the mass dissemination of computers and cell phones as their prices have fallen over time.

---

13. George Selgin, *Bank Deregulation and Monetary Order*, (London: Routledge, 1996)
14. The content in this section represents an edited transcription of the lecture cited in footnote 15. Quotation marks and indentations were not used to minimize excessive, distractive formatting. The three charts comparing the German stock market to the Dow Jones were taken from the article "*Zee Stabilitee & The Wealth Effect*" published anonymously at ZeroHedge.com on September 15, 2012.
15. Peter Schiff, "*What About Money Causes Economic Crises?*" Ron Paul Lecture Series (Washington D.C.), December 19, 2011

Now that the U.S. has a fiat currency, the Fed is able to and does send false signals to the market when it manipulates interest rates. As a result, investments are made that shouldn't be made. In other words, resources are misallocated. The booms are caused by this misallocation or mal-investment. For example, to avoid the corrections associated with the bursting of the dot-com bubble, the Fed inflated the housing bubble. When people buy houses, they buy them based on the monthly payment, which is a function of the mortgage rate. When the Fed sets interest rates at 1% leading banks to offer interest-only teaser rates on mortgages, it encourages people to become overly vested in real estate as opposed to employing their resources on more productive sectors of the economy. This real estate heavy economy was a function of money being too cheap. Instead of the market setting interest rates, central planners at the Fed picked rates.

When the housing bubble burst, President Bush blamed Wall Street for being drunk. They *were* drunk—on the liquor provided them by the Fed in the form of excessively low interest rates. A comparison can indeed be made between the tough choices required to allow an economy to correct and a drug rehab facility. When a patient checks in and is suffering from withdrawal, the rehab facility isn't happy to see the patient suffer, it's just a necessary aspect of the recovery process. If every time a drug addict checked into rehab, he was given drugs to minimize his suffering, the rehab facility might become a popular destination, but the patient would never be cured. When the narcotic of cheap money begins to wear off and interest rates begin to rise, the painful repercussions of the financial mistakes made during the boom begin to surface. The recession is where the mistakes are corrected; recession is needed to recover a healthy economy. Instead of suffering the full impact of the 2008 financial crisis as was needed for real economic recovery, the Fed has inflated a dollar bubble by disseminating over $16 trillion in financial institution bailouts around the world.

In addition to people who made bad investments during the boom losing money, people that have jobs as a result of the boom that shouldn't exist must lose those jobs so that they can be employed in a different, more productive capacity. Politicians most often don't differentiate between jobs. They think as long as people have a job, it's okay. If one person has a job digging a ditch and someone else has a job filling it in, then they're both employed, and that is good. It's not. There's nothing to show for the labor. Jobs are not the end; jobs are a means to the end. When people have a job, they want what they can buy with their paychecks, but there's only something to buy if something is produced. People have to be employed productively.

Why does the Fed pick such low rates? Politicians like the boom; everybody thinks the boom is good. When voters feel good, incumbents are more likely to get reelected. In addition to the problems caused directly by monetary policy, the Fed supports the politicians further by enabling irresponsible fiscal policy. Policymakers fail to acknowledge that the stimulus is what led to the recession. The minute recession hits, what does the government want to do? Create or expand government programs and benefits that can only be paid for by financing from the Fed, et al. Spending printed money helps the short-term picture and effectively buys votes because people still want their benefits. Everything that needs to be done for the economy is bad politics. These inflated bubbles and inevitable corrections known as the business cycle are exacerbated, if not created, by monetary and fiscal policy.

Meanwhile, the Keynesian perspective suits the politicians' needs perfectly. Keynesian economists say that there is not enough demand and that it's a good thing when prices go up; otherwise, there would be deflation. They advocate that if Americans are broke, more money needs to be printed, and the government needs to spend. Spend what? If the people are broke, then the government is broke. The people are broke because they're loaded up with debt, and they're not sufficiently productive. Where does the government get its money? Taxes on the production of its people.

This problem was highlighted in the late Soviet Union. The Soviets bragged that they had very low unemployment; everyone worked for the government. Their citizens would have to wait in line for six hours for a loaf of bread because no one was baking bread. Most of the population was working for the government making a paycheck but in an unproductive capacity. If no one is producing, then one's salary doesn't have any value; it's just paper. Governments can print money all of they want, but they can't print valuable production.

U.S. fiscal policy is designed to postpone the day of reckoning beyond the next election. If giving benefits such as unemployment grows the economy, then why limit it to the unemployed? Why not just give everyone money to scale the projected positive impact on the economy? Such programs don't grow the economy. Look at the debt and how it's grown much more than GDP. The illusion of growth is perpetuated by highlighting only half of the balance sheet. The result is that instead of the government taking the money from its citizens via taxation, it takes the spending power from their money via inflation. So they don't see the tax; they feel the tax. Financial bubbles such as what's been experienced in the stock market and housing are one expression of inflation. Another is manifest in increased grocery or energy prices. The government blames those increased prices on greedy oil companies, financial speculation, natural disasters, bad weather, etc. The real (adjusted for inflation) price of oil is now less than it was during the 1950s.

The U.S. government is enabled to perpetuate these problems to an extent greater than any other nation because the U.S. dollar remains the world reserve currency. Until WWII, all countries were on the gold standard. After WWII, the U.S. had nearly all of the world's gold. The U.S. got this gold from foreign countries buying the goods it produced. The U.S. became the world's most productive economy, despite having the world's highest-paid labor force, because it was the world's freest capitalistic society. U.S. workers were the most productive because of access to capital and limited government regulation. Fueled by being the world's leading economic power, the U.S. proposed a new monetary system where foreign central banks would back their currency by the U.S. dollar, which was, of course, backed by gold. If foreign banks held dollars, they received interest. If they held gold, they had storage costs. This was the crux of the Bretton Woods Agreement. Soon after, the U.S. abused this system by printing more money than it had in gold. Instead of allowing the dollar to correct, the U.S. defaulted by closing the gold window in 1971. The dollar was marked down by about 2/3 during the 1970s, but it remained the world's reserve currency. Oil went from $3 a barrel to $30 a barrel, and gold went from $35 per ounce to $800 per ounce. As a result of this inflation, the U.S. standard of living declined dramatically, and, not so coincidentally, women entered the workforce en masse.

Even though the world marked down the dollar, it stabilized when Fed Chairman Paul Volcker raised interest rates to over 20% in the early 1980s. Once the world realized the dollar was backed by nothing, however, it became much easier for the U.S. to run deficits because they no longer had to pretend the dollar was backed by the commensurate amount of gold. This was the beginning of the end of the U.S. as the world's biggest creditor and producer of high-quality, low-cost goods. The U.S went through a great transformation from then on as it began to live off the printing press. To cover for its lack of national production, the U.S simply borrows money from the Fed and foreign countries to support endless spending.

When the dollar can be printed out of thin air, and the world takes it, the U.S. can buy all of the products it needs from its trading partners for nothing. The Chinese invest land, labor, and capital making things for Americans in exchange for dollars that were simply run off the printing press. And the only thing they can do with them is loan them back to us buying Treasuries (i.e., more dollars). Many people misunderstand this relationship believing that the Chinese benefit from it. The Chinese aren't gaining nearly as much as the U.S. The U.S. gets all of the stuff, and the Chinese get all of the work. The U.S. says that the Chinese get jobs, but the slaves had jobs—that wasn't a very good deal for them.

The whole idea behind exporting is not to create jobs; it's to eliminate jobs. A country exports so that it can import something else; it's a means to maximize consumption. If there's something that one country makes better than others, it's most efficient for that country to focus on making that one thing and trading it for stuff that others make better. Currently, when the U.S. trades with foreign nations, they send the U.S. stuff, and the U.S. says it has nothing for them but an IOU (dollars). Our trade partners, such as China, take the dollars because it's the world's reserve currency. They think that one day that they'll use them to buy something, but the stuff the Chinese want to buy is all made in China.

The U.S. now has this entire bubble of a phony economy that is predicated on Americans borrowing money they didn't save to buy products they can't afford and didn't make. All of U.S. economic policy is designed to sustain this. As with all bubbles, it can't last forever, and corrections will occur. The longer the corrections are delayed by centrally planned policy, the bigger the corrections and the deeper the recession will be. Interest rates must rise if the economy is going to correct, but that will be extremely painful as the U.S. is so overly indebted. Without market-driven interest rates, the U.S. will never have a real recovery.

The bank stress test conducted by the Fed on the nineteen largest financial institutions in March 2012 did not include a scenario of an increase in the federal funds rate. Was this because the Fed thinks rates will never go up, or were they concerned about the banks' ability, or inability, to remain solvent becoming exposed? The Fed maintains that interest rates will not rise, but it's impossible that interest rates will never rise. What happens when interest rates do go up? The reason the U.S. is able to pay the interest on its debt is that rates are so low. Banks are going to fail, housing is going to go down, the government will have to reduce spending drastically, and in fact, it may have to default on the bonds it's already sold. Who's going to save money (i.e., buy U.S. Treasuries) that's losing its value at an accelerating rate? Inflation is already substantially higher than what the Bureau of Labor Statistics ("BLS") reports via its "core" Consumer Pricing Index ("CPI"). The CPI is designed to make inflation appear low because food and energy were removed in 1980. Eventually, inflation will be so pronounced that the government will be unable to ignore it, and interest rates are going to rise. When interest rates rise, the banks will fail again, except this time the government won't have the ability to bail them out. The next time the banks fail, the depositors will lose money. If the government can't cover its own debts, how can it bail out the FDIC? The U.S. is one chapter behind Europe.

When the housing bubble first began to crack in the subprime market, all of the experts from the Bush Administration down to Wall Street were on TV reassuring everyone it was contained. They said it was a tiny little problem, and the market was sound. The Austrian economists were saying that the problem was not just a subprime problem, it was a mortgage problem. It's not a matter of contagion; everybody is already sick; it's just a matter of time before the symptoms show up.

Now, it's the same issue with sovereign debt. This is not an Italian, Greek, or Spanish problem; it's a debt problem, and the U.S has more debt than Europe. The government bubble is the biggest yet, and it is not sustainable. Eventually, the Fed will be the only market for American debt as trade partners such as China witness their current holdings deteriorate under inflationary pressures. The real crisis that the U.S. is at great risk of experiencing is a sovereign debt crisis, a collapse of the bond market and a collapse of the dollar on a much grander scale than is being seen in Europe. The U.S., having the world's reserve currency, ability to print money, and support of Keynesian propaganda, doesn't make it immune indefinitely to the real laws of macroeconomics.

EFFECTS OF U.S. MONETARY POLICY ON THE GREATER ECONOMY

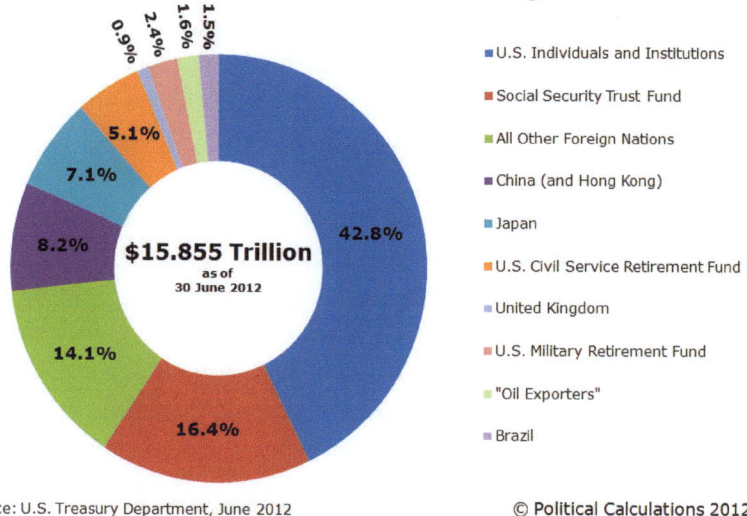

This chart identifies the creditors of the U.S. government as a percentage of total U.S. government debt as of June 2012.

Some advocate that increasing taxes is the way to fix the problem. The U.S has borrowed more money than its citizens could possibly repay. Raising taxes on the top 1%–10%, or even the top 99%, will not come close to eliminating the debt. It will have to come through either a restructuring or default. There are two ways in which this can come to fruition. One, Congress can level with its creditors and say it can't pay 100 cents on the dollar on its outstanding Treasuries and level with people expecting government benefits by means-testing to make do with less. The second way is to inflate the currency into oblivion, at which time the dollar will not only not be worth a Continental, it won't be worth a Federal Reserve Note. The U.S. will not be able to roll over its debt continually. Eventually, its creditors will want to get paid, and the U.S. can't pay. The U.S. government is not going to do the right thing until there is a crisis. There is a phony crisis every time the Congress is forced to raise the debt ceiling, which tells its creditors that it's running a Ponzi Scheme. The U.S. doesn't say it will cut spending or raise taxes to cover its obligations; the U.S. says that if it can't borrow more money, it can't pay who it already owes. At some point, U.S. lenders will stop raising the credit ceiling. One way or another, the people who have loaned money to the U.S. will lose. The longer these mal-investments pile up, the bigger the collapse and the harder it will be to restore economic balance. Right now, Europe is buying the U.S. time as their situation, for the time being, is relatively worse.

All of these problems result from government and their intervention into free markets mixing capitalism with socialism. Then, of course, the government turns around and blames capitalism, proposing that further government intervention is required to solve the problem. The real threat to liberty is that this is such an enormous problem that the U.S. could end up with total government. The solutions are in the market: letting the corrections take place, returning to economic equilibrium, and suffering the short-term consequences.

EFFECTS OF U.S. MONETARY POLICY ON THE GREATER ECONOMY,

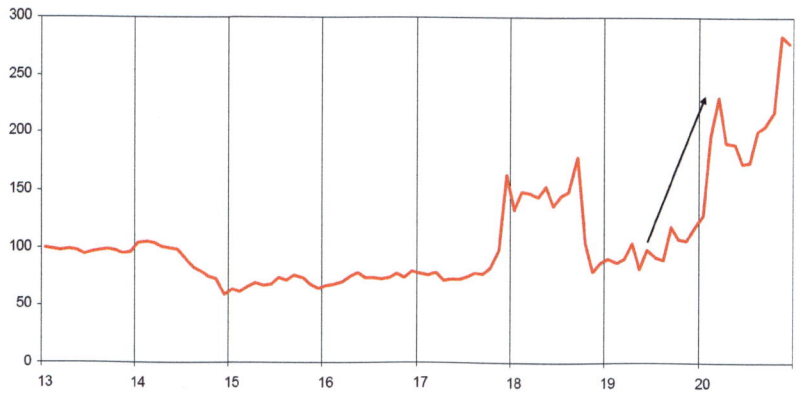

This chart illustrates the nominal price of the German stock market from 1914 to 1927.

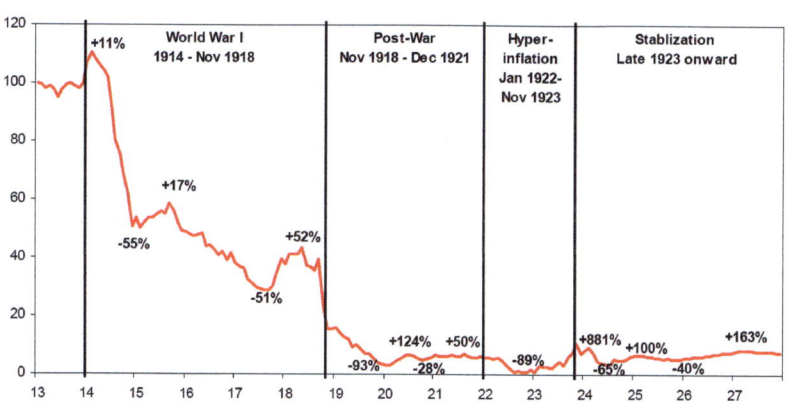

This chart illustrates the real value of the German stock market from 1914 to 1927.

PROLOGUE: DECIPHERING MONETARY POLICY

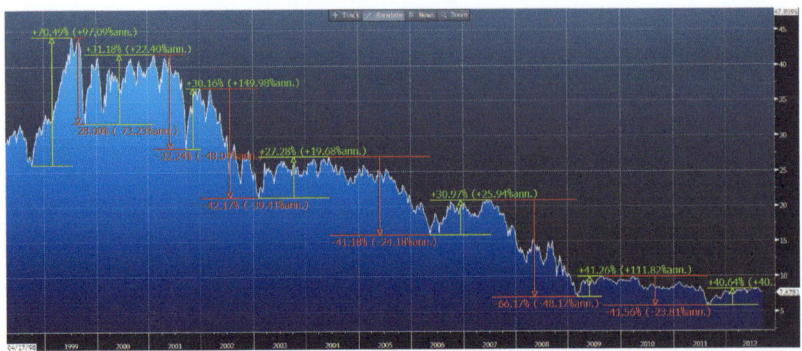

This chart illustrates the real value of the Dow Jones Industrial Average from 1999 to present (*adjusted for the value of gold*).

MOVING AGAINST THE MARKET MOVERS

If one assumes that monetary policy will not result in meaningful long-term economic recovery, then long-term "investment markets" ought not to respond positively to it. The securities markets, both fixed income and equities, are, at least in the short term, detached from value fundamentals while being attached to the supply of currency held in the banking system. For the overwhelming majority of traders, making predictions of their future movement is more a game of speculation than that of responsible investing.

One of the most popular alternatives to the securities markets has been gold. At $1,781 per ounce, the estimated supply of the world's gold at 165,000 metric tons[16] is valued at $9,018,526,495,604. While gold and silver have historically been recognized as money, it is not necessary for the world's supply of gold to reflect the value of the world's GDP. Gold is simply one commodity among many resources that contribute to the world's total asset value. While the price of gold is likely to continue rising as people hedge against inflationary risk, a better value will likely be available in other precious metals, if not other nonfinancial

---

16. "About gold > Demand and supply". Retrieved October 1, 2012. (http://www.gold.org/about_gold/story_of_gold/demand_and_supply)

assets altogether. For example, gold currently runs at about 50 times the price of silver. Historically, the gold to silver price ratio had been approximately 16:1 until gold began to wildly outrun silver just after the Civil War.

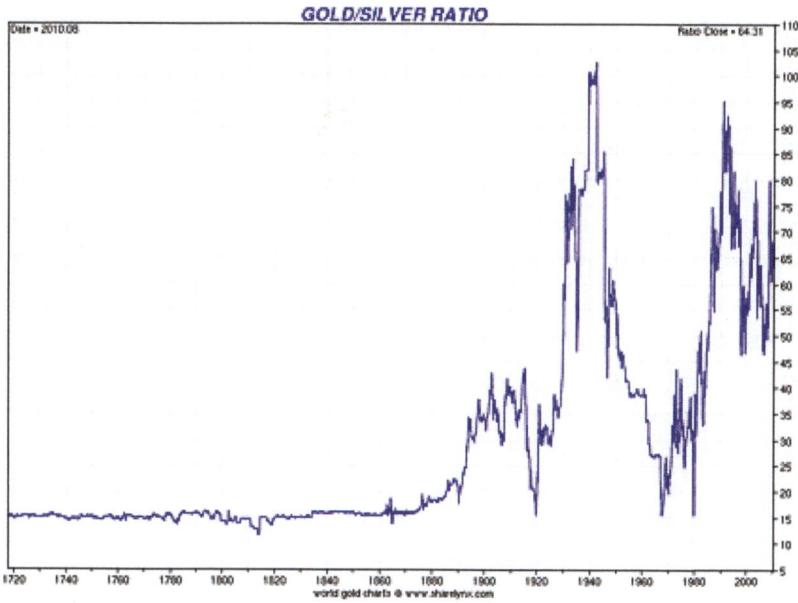

This graph illustrates the gold to silver price ratio from 1720 to 2010.

While gold does represent a potentially high degree of safety in terms of capital preservation, it is important to consider the price of other commodities or hard assets when evaluating quality alternatives to publicly traded stocks and bonds—and other asset classes altogether, for that matter.

Commodities aren't the panacea they may seem to be at first glance. There are holding or storage costs to consider that detract from potential appreciation, and unlike other asset classes, commodities are not capable of generating any income to offset those costs. So, while it's good to own precious metals in particular, they should probably not exceed any more than 10% of your overall holdings unless you absolutely know that a total economic collapse is imminent. Unfortunately, precisely timing such things is nigh impossible.

So, people commonly turn to real estate. Real estate is great. The problem with real estate, however, is that its performance is subject to the expertise and effort of its management, which more often than not is sorely lacking as we'll discuss later.

All the while, Treasuries actually generate negative real yield (real yield is nominal or stated yield minus inflation), and cash quickly loses purchasing power as it sits idle.

So, what's left to do? Publicly traded assets are unpredictably volatile; physical commodity prices are manipulated and generate negative cash flow; and real estate has demonstrated that, like stocks, it's also subject to market crashes, and it's managed by a culture that lacks the critical financial expertise required to navigate such economic crises successfully.

This book is going to show you exactly how to successfully navigate this seemingly impossible gauntlet and quickly rise to the top of the economic food chain with the extraordinarily powerful Shadow Banker's Secrets.

Preface

Source: Walt Handelsman, Newsday.

THE GOLDEN RULE: WHOEVER ~~HAS THE GOLD~~ UNDERSTANDS MONEY MAKES THE RULES

To grow, scale and protect your investment portfolio or business at the level we're discussing in this book, we have to understand the source of all money as we know it: banks.

Most people hold the belief that whoever has the gold makes the rules. This is absolutely not true. The reality is that whoever understands money makes the rules, and once you understand the mechanics of banking, the truth of this statement becomes absolutely clear.

As we covered within the prologue, the money that banks use and profit from is not theirs. Retail, commercial, and shadow banks effectively use the money of their depositors, investors, and their central bank to finance others. The unique quality they possess that affords them their station in the economy is a thorough understanding of the mechanics of money and their perceived ability to manage risk. Chasing money itself without an understanding of how it's created is a never-ending rat race that will always leave you at the feet of someone else who controls more.

The second step to success in the investment business en route to the top of the economic food chain is understanding how the banking system literally creates money and assets out of thin air, albeit with some constraint, so that you can legally do the same. I'm going to show you how.

WHAT IS A SHADOW BANK?

The term is featured in the title of this book, but what exactly is a shadow bank? Shadow banks are similar to any other bank except they generally don't deal with the public directly, they are subject to far less regulation, and they have the potential to be far more profitable.

The shadow banking system (or shadow financial system) is a network of financial institutions comprised of non-depository banks (e.g., investment banks, hedge funds, structured investment vehicles, money market funds, and other non-bank financial institutions).

Shadow banks are called such because they operate outside—in the shadows of—the regulatory framework that governs depository institutions.

Shadow banking institutions generally serve as intermediaries between investors and capital seekers creating debt and equity for high-net-worth individuals ("HNWI"), institutional investors, and corporations, and profiting from fees and/or from arbitrage in investment yields.

How would your portfolio or business change if you were your own shadow bank and able to provide yourself access to as much capital as you could responsibly use? The purpose of this book is to show you how to do just that while being fully compliant with all relevant laws and regulations.

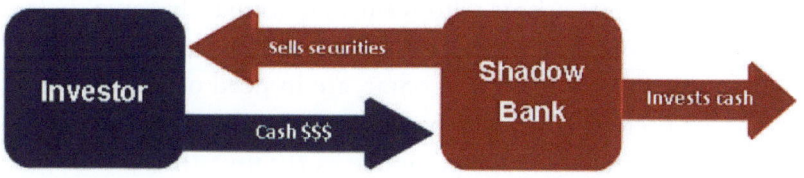

The dynamic between investors and shadow banks.

One point to make clear for non-financial professionals, real estate and retail investors who may not yet be familiar with financial services lingo: alternative assets are anything that are not stocks, bonds, or cash equivalents, which means that real estate falls squarely under the category of alternative assets. So, when I say alternatives, I'm including real estate.

WHO IS THIS FOR?

That being said, who is this for?

1. Alternative investment managers, including hedge fund managers, real estate investors, asset managers, lenders, and syndicators, (new or seasoned) who want to protect their business from the next market crash and/or who want access to unlimited capital to execute their investment business on their own terms

2. Retail investors and savers (those who aren't financial experts, such as retirees) who have a nest egg from which they need to generate decent income or growth, but who can't afford much risk exposure and who want to meaningfully improve their portfolio and/or replace their financial advisor

3. Financial professionals who want to scale their business and create competitive advantage by incorporating reliable, quantifiable investment risk measures and alternative assets that generate demonstrably superior risk-adjusted performance into their practice

4. Real estate agents who want to compliantly serve their investor-clients in search of returns that are not available via the MLS or CoStar, are in need of 1031 assets or prefer quality passive investment opportunities, and who want to develop a niche as *the* investment real estate consultant in their market

5. Independent insurance agents, IRA custodians, accountants, or attorneys who want to compliantly serve their clients in need of better investment options than what they are being offered by their financial advisors or otherwise have available through their retirement accounts

6. Marketers and relationship builders who want to serve and monetize their network by compliantly providing exclusive access to high-quality alternative investments (like top-performing hedge funds)

I know quite a few of you are already successful syndicators, and you may be tempted to believe that represents the ceiling for your business. It's not.

SYNDICATORS VS. FINANCIAL INSTITUTIONS

There are subtle but very important distinctions to make between legitimate shadow banking financial institutions and syndicators who raise money for real estate, energy projects, or otherwise on a deal-by-deal basis. These distinctions allow financial institutions to access the capital markets in ways syndicators can only dream of. In other words, these distinctions are some of the biggest reasons why credible financial advisors won't even consider working with most syndicators in their effort to raise money. Here's a brief comparison:

	Not a Financial Institution	Financial Institutions		
	SYNDICATIONS	HEDGE FUNDS	PRIVATE EQUITY FUNDS	INVESTMENT BANKS
WHAT?	Sell Closed-End Partnership Interests (Shares) in a Project	Sell Open-End Partership Interests (Shares) in a Strategy Based upon a Portfolio of Equities & Derivatives	Sell Closed-End Partnership Interests (Shares) in a Strategy Based upon a Portfolio of Companies	Sell Securities They Underwrite
HOW?	Sell a Story Predicting Future Performance Based on the Market	Sell Market-Neutral Historical Performance	Sell Ability to Turnaround/Grow Companies & Exit	Sell Expected Performance of Securities Issues
WHO?	Sell Their Private Issues to Individuals Based Upon Personal/Trust-Based Relationships	Sell Their Private Issues to Sophisticated/Institutional Investors Based Upon Merit	Sell Their Private Issues to Sophisticated/Institutional Investors Based Upon Merit	Sell Structured Products & Client Company Issues to Sales & Trading Clients' Specific Appetites
WHY?	Profit (and Crash) with the Market	Profit from Its Ability to Generate Consistently Strong Performance Regardless of the Market	Profit from Its Ability to Generate Consistently Strong Performance Regardless of the Market	Profit from Advisory Fees & the Broker-Dealer Function

Syndicators chase "investors".   Financial institutions sell sought-after financial products.

Syndications, financial institutions, and their characteristics.

How nice would it be to go from being the syndicator begging for money with each new deal to becoming the financial institution who can say, "I'll take the money you're trying to throw at me when I feel like it, but I don't need it right now"? If you're not sure, I'll tell you: It's nice.

"I found Ben's discourse on investment banking to be very informative and valuable. He provides a new way to look at investing."

FRANK GUTTA, CPA, is the managing partner of Gutta, Sharfi & Co. CPAs. He has been in practice as a tax and financial expert for over 30 years.

I know that some of you are credentialed professionals who aren't new to investing and have quite a bit of experience with alternative assets, so I thought the previous statement by Frank, who is a CPA and runs a successful financial planning business, was important to highlight as a testament to the comprehensive nature of the subject matter covered in this book. My goal is to provide you with valuable, actionable items that all financial professionals and investors can use to scale their businesses and portfolios dramatically. Alternative assets are just a tool, and to date, a grossly underutilized and misused one.

YOUR GOALS & MY OBJECTIVE

So, to what extent do you want to scale? What do you need to retire comfortably, to own your time and live your life without compromise? How much money do you need to fulfill your business's potential? $10 million? $100 million? $1 billion? $100 billion?

Are you a multifamily syndicator who wants to become the dominant player in your MSA or even nationally? How much money do you need to accomplish that? Are you a financial advisor working to scale past $1 billion in assets under management ("AUM")?

Are you just starting out as a real estate investor and need available capital to flip houses in your local area? Are you a private lender wanting to achieve institutional scale?

Are you an emerging hedge fund manager striving to reach Ray Dalio status?

Are you a retail investor just looking for a comfortable, stress-free retirement?

While it may sound like fluff—largely because of all of the insincere people pushing the idea—it is important to clearly identify your ultimate goals without fear of failure and visualize the details of achieving them.

We used visualization in my days as both a college and professional athlete, and its value holds in whatever goal you're working to achieve. Not only does it remind us of what we're working for (a sort of motivational tool) but it also helps build belief and expectation that the goal can and will be achieved." I think this quote that was frequently echoed by one of the best coaches and most successful people of all-time—Skip Bertman of LSU, who won five national championships over a ten-year span—really sums it up:

> *"Anything you vividly imagine, ardently desire, sincerely believe, and enthusiastically act upon must inevitably come to pass."*

The key word here is *anything*. While this image shows a pile of money, your vision of success can be anything. The point is that you need to make an effort to formulate a clear vision of what your success looks like. With that being said, how much capital do you need to achieve your professional and financial goals and ultimately fulfill your potential?

This is what $1,000,000,000 in cash looks like.

Once we've identified what we want, we now have to dive into the how. What is your exact plan to achieve your goals?

While vision is an important step, it's only the first one. Next, we have to achieve belief. True belief, as opposed to hope, can only fully form as vision evolves into a mission, as specific goals and objectives grow into something we can begin to enthusiastically act upon, ultimately implementing the strategy and tactics that will get us where we have decided to be with consistency. Belief is forged by repetition.

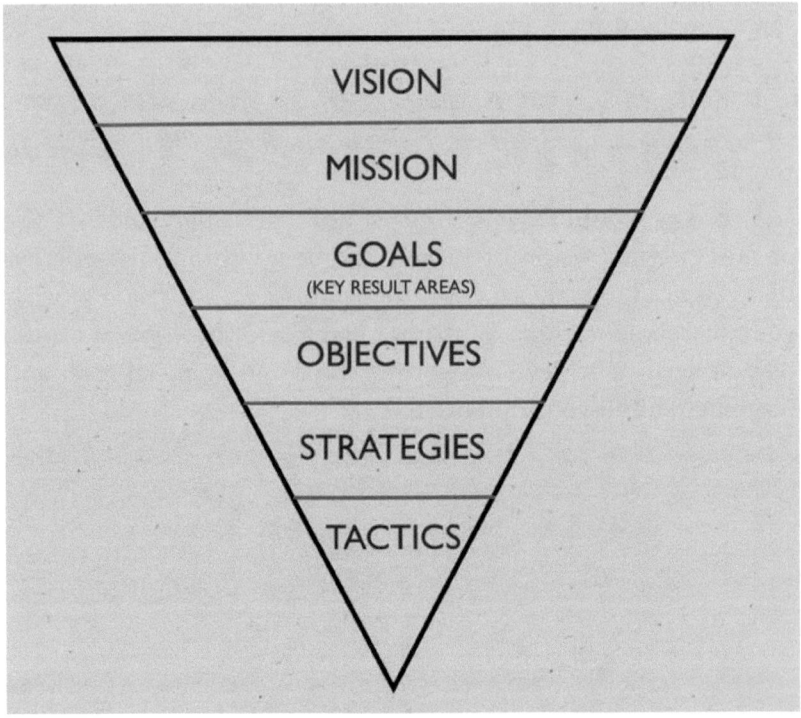

The success funnel.

I know a lot of you are already successful in your own right, but to achieve a truly uncompromised level of success means to take on new goals, new skills, and new efforts. In some respects, this can be more difficult than what was required even to get where you are. We're talking about becoming leaders in value creation and taking on a great deal of misguided cultural inertia in the process. That being said, I've successfully done it, and whether you're a real estate investor, an attorney, a financial advisor, or otherwise—you can too.

I want to set clear expectations. My goal for this book is to demonstrate the following:

The only way to achieve complete financial independence is to possess the ability to create and control unlimited capital.

The only way to acquire the ability to create and control unlimited capital is through the closely guarded secrets of the shadow banking system that I reveal in this book.

As I said previously, we're going to discuss exactly how you can effectively issue and control your own money.

> *"Permit me to issue and control the money of a nation, and I care not who makes its laws."*
>
> Mayer Amschel Rothschild,
> attributed by Gertrude M. Coogan (1935)

Continuing with a little more detailed look at my objectives for this book, I will:

1. Reveal how to choose, and even create, investments that generate strong returns even when the markets take a hit. In other words, I show you how to consistently achieve better risk-adjusted returns than what is otherwise available through the public capital markets (i.e., stock and bond markets), traditional real estate investing, or even crowdfunding.

2. Open your eyes to how you can use these investment management skills to meet the approximately $20 trillion demand of other investors in desperate need of strong, risk-adjusted returns. In other words, I show you how to raise unlimited capital by issuing private securities that compete with the best hedge funds in the world.

3. Demonstrate how you can use your unique resources and skillset to profit as an investment professional, whether you are the technical expert who can create great risk-adjusted investment returns (for yourself or others) or the relationship builder who can aggregate capital.

There are a few people—especially traditionally-oriented financial planners, insurance, and real estate agents—who are going to see the topics covered in this book as somewhat unfamiliar and complex and will want to stop reading. Trust me when I tell you this stuff is for you, and you probably need it more than anyone else. You're stuck in a field that is forced to sell the same exact products and services in the exact same way as thousands of other brokers and agents in completely flooded markets. I implore you to overcome that knee-jerk reaction and open your mind to the possibilities that are available to you by taking advantage of the untapped resources at your disposal and looking at things from a slightly different perspective.

To provide some context with respect to the value contained within this book, for us to refine, structure, and capitalize our clients' alternative asset management businesses, it costs them a minimum of $750,000, and for more complex solutions, costs can exceed $5,000,000. However, it's important to note that all upfront fees paid by our clients are reimbursed by the structures we create. The result is that our clients ultimately incur no expense to have us scale their business to 9-figures plus, but the point is that they're still fronting $750,000 or more for the very same information you're getting in this book.

Now, I know $750,000 sounds like a lot of money (and it is) but if I could prove to you that our process would provide your business with $100,000,000 plus, wouldn't you be willing to pay $750,000? It's like putting one dollar in a change machine that spits out $133 in return. What I'm providing you in this book is the means to build your own money creating machine.

All that being said—and somewhat tongue in cheek—don't use what you're going to learn here to become just another evil bankster. As the old adage goes, "With great power comes great responsibility." For centuries, we've seen these esoteric skills used to enslave nations, but there's absolutely no good reason to use what I cover in this book for anything other than to create substantial wealth for both yourself and your investors by running a good business. The first step to success in the investment business is to competently protect other people's money with even more tenacity than you do your own.

Don't be myopic... while many people in a position of financial strength tend to abuse that power, it is more profitable—and fulfilling—to be ethical.

Just in case it's not obvious already, what I'm introducing in this book is like nothing you've ever seen—whether you're a financial advisor with a billion-dollar AUM or real estate guru—and the reason for sharing Ryan's comments below is to highlight this fact. Ryan runs one of the most sophisticated real estate investment associations in the country and is now president of the National Real Estate Investors Association; I have a great deal of respect for him. So, for him to say:

"Every time I talk to Ben about money, finance, risk, and investment in real estate, I always learn something new. He's incredibly insightful."

RYAN KUHLMAN is the owner and president of the Broward and Miami-Dade Real Estate Investors Associations and president of the National Real Estate Investors Association. He has been involved in real estate since 1990.

That means something.

I also share Ryan's comments to help set expectations. This subject matter is fairly complicated, but it's not beyond the reach of new investors, agents, and financial professionals who are smart and driven.

You can use the secrets we're about to discuss to simply improve the performance of your personal investment portfolio or to create millions, if not billions of dollars, running your own firm. But as you might expect, the bigger your goals, the more commitment and effort that are required to achieve them.

BEN SUMMERS & ADAGIO GROUP

When I started out as a professional investor in 2005, my goal was to simply run a business to replace my income as a corporate employee. The more work I completed toward each successive goal along my path, however, the more money and professional pride I saw could be attained. My motivation and commitment grew commensurately, and I expect the same will happen for you.

These pictures of my beautiful significant other, Daniela, with me; my adorable daughter, Lauren; and this group shot at a polo match in Wellington begin to capture why it's worth it to me. Making an effort to be able to literally dictate my net worth provided a conduit to doing great things with great people and the ability to have the life I want on my terms with the people I love. The same effort applied to what I'm sharing with you today can provide you with the same results.

I am going to take a few minutes here to introduce myself and go over how I arrived where I am now. There are a couple reasons for doing so: First, it's important to see that you don't have to have an Ivy League MBA and be a Goldman Sachs alum to operate at the top of the finance game successfully. Second, my background serves as a practical reference for you to get to where you want to be no matter where in your journey you are right now. It demonstrates that the places you're going to find the most valuable lessons are not where you'd typically think to look or where others might expect.

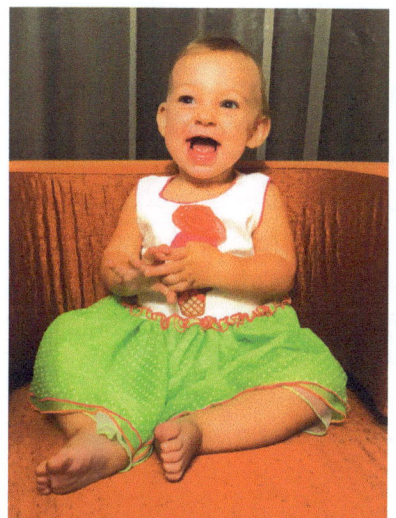

Top Left: Lauren Summers at one year old; Top Right: Daniela and Ben Summers; Bottom: Ben Summers and friends celebrating a season-ending polo match in Wellington, Florida.

I am the founder and managing director of Adagio Group. I grew up just outside of Baton Rouge, Louisiana with one single passion: to be a successful athlete. And relatively speaking, I was. I overcame a "career-ending" shoulder injury and surgery in high school to have the opportunity to play both football and baseball as a quarterback and pitcher at the Division 1A level in college. I went on to sign with the San Diego Padres organization, was an opening day starter, and won a minor league championship. Since then, I've also had the chance to work side-by-side with Hall of Fame wide receiver, Cris Carter, and other greats to train prospective high-round draft picks for the NFL combine in preparation for the draft.

As my baseball career was winding down, I finished up my degree at LSU. I majored in physics and studied music (piano performance, music theory, and composition) as a second discipline. When baseball was finally over, the next biggest challenge was to find something else that would get me as motivated as sports had. I was miserable in my new existence that was little more than a hunt to pay rent and bills. As a default, my post-athletic career started as an engineer in the oil and gas services industry. My first stop was a one-year stint in Houston building refinery additions for Shell, then I moved on to developing Shell's natural gas infrastructure in West Africa before finally moving to Northern Europe where I split my time between Aberdeen, Scotland and Stavanger, Norway, bringing new drilling technologies to the global upstream market.

I learned a lot about the nature of corporate business during that time, but the most valuable lesson I learned was that subjecting myself to the political bureaucracy of corporate life was no way to live. Don't get me wrong, there was some really great stuff about that experience, not the least of which was being able to travel the world with a seemingly endless expense account, but I was owned, and that was something I could not abide. My oil and gas experience had uncovered a new passion—the pursuit of financial independence—so I decided to go out on my own.

Clockwise from Top Left: Ben Summers and his grandfather James Hoover during warmups before the 2001 LSU Baseball Alumni Game; Ben graduating from LSU in physics; Ben celebrating winning the 2001 AAA championship; Ben pitching; Ben sailing the Norwegian fjords; Ben cross-country skiing in Norway; the Continuous Circulation System, one of the drilling technologies Ben helped bring to market in Europe; Ben and friends at the Airport Hotel in Port Harcourt, Nigeria; Offshore Gas Gathering System construction on Bonny Island, Nigeria; gates of the Wilbros compound in Choba, Nigeria; military escort for transit between Choba and Bonny Island.

I knew that one of the biggest challenges in starting a new business was start-up capital, and of all of the industries to get into, real estate investing provided the greatest opportunity for leverage, which minimized the start-up capital burden. Once the decision to pursue investment real estate was made, I spent all my spare time in the waning days of my energy services career reading everything I could get my hands on that discussed the topic of real estate investing.

You may find it surprising that I think Carleton Sheets' *No Down Payment* course was by far the most comprehensive and valuable information on the subject available at that time, and it probably still is today. I find it disappointing that so many people dismissed his content. I suspect that the typical corporate employee is unconsciously trained to value a very narrow marketing approach that is dependent upon well-established branding. One thing I can attest to is that corporate indoctrination instills a false sense of confidence in ignorance that makes moderately successful people highly overly confident in what they know and averse to the information they often need the most. I think that dynamic highlights the need for and value of a book like this one as a necessary tool to re-educate the market on how to adopt innovation as a means to create value.

Top Left: How to Buy Your First Home or Investment Property with No Down Payment by Carleton Sheets;
Top Right: Creative Real Estate Online; Bottom: Hard money lending.

With that, Adagio, LLC was born in Houston, Texas on May 11, 2005 as a single-entity real estate investment company that operated in both Florida and Texas.

It didn't take long after diving into real estate investing, however, to realize that there are not very many truly good deals available at any given time, and there are a lot of deep-pocketed, well-established investors chasing them. The result is that most new investors are stuck either overpaying for assets or experiencing very limited deal flow.

Another thing I discovered was much more encouraging: the hard money lender. It was immediately clear that these lenders had the best perch of everyone playing the real estate game. Not only were there an endless stream of deals being brought to them, but their returns were in the high teens, and they had a significant equity cushion protecting their position. That's the perch upon which I quickly moved to position Adagio.

The only problem with becoming a lender is that it takes a lot of liquid capital to execute—much more than I had at the time. To successfully transition Adagio from a real estate acquisition to a real estate lending firm, I would have to raise money from others. While this is not an easy task, the good news is that there's an entire sector of the economy dedicated to this endeavor: financial services. To be successful, I would have to learn the business of finance—and that's what I did.

The first move I made was to bring in Karl Moore, who not only holds a securities law degree from Vanderbilt but has also worked as an investment analyst for a range of hedge funds and investment banks. Together, we developed Adagio into a formal fund manager, positioning us to launch an asset-based lending, or ABL, fund. Meanwhile, I dove into the best finance texts available, including the CFA manuals and Nassim Taleb's *Incerto* (paying special attention to tail risk management). I explored the application of my mathematical physics skills to quantitative finance, pored over all of the federal securities laws, and acquired the FINRA Series 65 License along the way.

PREFACE

Annual Returns			
	ABL	S&P 500	MSCI US REIT
2007	26.32%	5.49%	-16.82%
2008	32.07%	-37.00%	-37.97%
2009	41.56%	26.46%	28.61%
2010	26.32%	15.06%	28.48%
2011	27.71%	2.11%	8.69%
2012	33.36%	16.00%	17.77%
2013	25.96%	32.39%	2.47%
2014	20.93%	13.69%	30.38%
2015	27.26%	1.38%	25.20%
Average *	28.94%	6.40%	6.92%

Top Left: Ben Summers and Karl Moore;
Top Right: Securities Act of 1933 snippet;
Bottom Right: CFA Institute's Quantitative Investment Analysis textbook;
Adagio ABL, S&P 500 and MSCI US REIT Indices annual returns.

In addition to the general finance knowledge I acquired with that effort, I uncovered what is arguably the most important graph any real estate market participant could ever get its hands on. It was a graph of BLS and FHFA data that illustrated how real estate could be managed to consistently generate double-digit returns no matter what the market was doing. This new insight was tested with the 2008 financial crisis, and it passed with flying colors—but more on that later.

To this day, I continue to be awestruck by how far ahead my independent study has put me relative to almost everyone I meet who has been formally trained in finance and has spent years at one of the big wirehouses. The lesson is that when you learn something because you want to, as opposed to because you have to, and because you see the direct benefit it will afford you, the more it will stick with you. You'll integrate what you've learned into how you think and make decisions. Knowledge becomes far more than something purely academic that is required to be regurgitated solely for the purpose of passing an exam. Knowledge becomes the foundation and means of your profitability.

In other words, passing on an Ivy League MBA or that entry-level analyst position at Goldman Sachs does not seal your fate or limit your potential. You can read a book without the supervision of faculty; you can do work without a boss; and it all still counts, potentially more so. The information you need and the work required to achieve anything in life exists independently of the medium through which it is delivered. You are able to learn everything you need to rise to the top of any profession at any time and from any place. All you really need is the will to do so.

As I mentioned previously, raising money is not easy for a small asset management firm (and by small, I mean managing under $100 million in assets), even when you do know the game. In fact, the more you know, the more you realize how constrained you are as a legitimate private fund manager in your efforts to raise capital.

As a circuitous means to get our message to the market and establish credible brand awareness, I developed a comprehensive course that distilled everything both passive and active investors need to know about finance and real estate so they'd be able to take advantage of the best of both worlds. I called it the *Accredited Investment Professional* or *AIP* course. In addition to helping students achieve their individual investment goals, the *AIP* course served us in a few different ways as well:

1. It educated potential borrows to help them become better positioned to borrow from us.

2. It educated potential investors in our fund on how to evaluate and compare both public and private investment opportunities.

3. It helped us establish pre-existing relationships with those potential fund investors so that we could maintain

our Reg D, Rule 506(b) exempt status, which prohibits general solicitation.

One day, I received an inquiry that seemed a little different from the others. Our course marketing had landed in the hands of a multifamily, deep value-add operator who was in desperate need of help. They were being investigated by several states in addition to the SEC for illegal fundraising activities, and to make matters worse, their portfolio was insolvent, meaning they owed their debt investors more than their assets were worth. Later, you'll have an opportunity to access this case study that anonymously details the circumstances and the mechanics of how we rescued this firm from the brink of bankruptcy and prison to compliantly and profitably raising approximately $5 million a month. To summarize, after a year of working to restructure their capital stack and methods of raising money, Adagio came out having evolved from fund manager to de facto boutique investment bank.

Adagio's Investment Banking for Alternatives.

I should note that, legally speaking, Adagio is an investment adviser only and not a broker-dealer, which means that in the strict technical sense, we are not an investment bank as defined in most legal contexts. Regardless of the semantics, we have developed a relationship with Morgan Stanley's New York office and work with other broker-dealers to compliantly provide de facto boutique investment banking services for potentially best-in-class alternative investment managers, such as real estate investors and emerging hedge fund managers, allowing them the unique opportunity to quickly scale from start-up to nine-figures plus in assets under management, or AUM, in a turnkey capacity.

What do boutique investment banks do? Well, they can do a lot of different things, and each one has generally carved out its own niche. To provide some context, this is what we do and what I'm going to be teaching each of you how to accomplish for yourselves today:

Alternative asset managers and sponsors: We help alternative asset managers (such as real estate syndicators and hedge fund managers) quickly raise hundreds of millions of dollars by measuring, improving, and communicating the risk-adjusted performance of their investment model, packaging it under an institutional-grade fund and distributing that fund through the appropriate capital markets channels to meet demand.

Licensed financial professionals: We help financial professionals quickly and compliantly grow their client base and reduce regulatory risk by definitively (quantifiably) measuring the risk characteristics of any asset (including alternatives) and providing all of their clients (including non-accredited investors) access to transparent, institutional-grade private structured products that generate better risk-adjusted performance than what's otherwise available through the capital markets (by taking advantage of inefficiencies in private markets that provide unique arbitrage opportunities via best-in-class asset managers).

Retail investors: We give retail investors peace of mind, knowing they can retire comfortably by definitively measuring the risk associated with all of their investments (from stocks, bonds, and mutual funds to hedge funds and real estate), objectively evaluating their financial advisor, and providing exclusive access to better risk-adjusted investment performance than what's otherwise only available to the top 0.1%.

Financial professionals (without FINRA licenses): We help financial professionals without FINRA licenses (accountants, attorneys, IRA custodians, marketers, etc.) quickly grow and monetize their client base by compliantly providing them exclusive access to the best risk-adjusted investment performance available (via institutional-grade private-structured products) that is otherwise reserved for the top 0.1%.

Regulatory and trade association professionals: We help regulatory and trade association professionals protect the investing public and support financial service professionals by providing education and guidance on quantitative risk analysis and relevant institutional-grade standards for alternative sponsors and asset managers.

I've just spent a fair amount of time talking about how to rise to the top of the finance industry from both a performance and regulatory perspective, but what makes me qualified to do so?

Here, you can see from FINRA's IARD system that I'm the managing director of Adagio Capital Management, which is an SEC-reporting investment adviser. Our CRD number is 286138; feel free to look us up through FINRA's BrokerCheck. Adagio has been in the business of private alternative asset management, fund management and helping other firms navigate the minefield of capital formation since 2005, and we've continued to grow and develop in complexity since that time as you can see in the timeline. Everything we do is in the public record as reported on our annual Form ADV submissions to the SEC through FINRA.

Top: Adagio Capital Management's IARD profile; Bottom: Adagio Group timeline.

Probably most valuable, however, is the application of my academic background in physics to quantitative finance. There aren't a whole lot of quants to be found operating outside the gates of the big box firms, but I'm one of them, and I'm providing that skill set to you with the sole intent of leveling the playing field and bringing merit-based decision-making tools to the market. As an example, I've developed a proprietary risk-rating matrix that consolidates the most informative risk-adjusted performance metrics into one user-friendly output that accounts for all four statistical moments of risk. It's like the Morningstar for alternatives, except the calculations are much more robust, but I'll go into that a little later once we've established the groundwork for risk analysis.

In short, everything I'm prescribing for you is exactly what we've done ourselves, and it's consistently proven over the last decade to be dramatically better than the run-of-the-mill approach.

That was a lot to go over, so here's a snapshot summarizing where that breadth and depth of experiences has landed me:

Benjamin D. Summers

- Managing Director of ADAGIO GROUP Since 2005 *(Generated Consistently High Returns Including 2008)*
- Executive Director of ADAGIO INSTITUTE, INC., a 501(c)(3) Public Charity
- Former Global Energy Services Executive *(Based in Houston, West Africa & Northern Europe)*
- Retired Professional Athlete *(Baseball)*
- Bachelor of Science in Physics, Studied Music as a Second Discipline (LSU)
- FINRA Series 65 License
- Florida Real Estate License

If you only take away one thing, remember that we were able to generate high, double-digit returns across the financial crisis of 2008 when just about everyone else was losing approximately 50% of their net worth, and we've continued to do so since then. Let that sink in for a minute…

It's worth noting that unlike most industries, financial advisors are severely limited by the SEC in terms of being able to offer testimonials and advertising, so there's not much we can disclose in terms of past clients, but you'll see as we move on how the information we go over very much stands on its own.

NO TESTIMONIALS & ADVERTISING PAST RESULTS

SEC rule 206(4)-1(a)(1) applies to investment advisors and by extension their representatives and reads as follows: "a. It shall constitute a fraudulent, deceptive, or manipulative act, practice, or course of business within the meaning of section 206(4) of the Act for any investment adviser registered or required to be registered under section 203 of the Act, directly or indirectly, to publish, circulate, or distribute any advertisement: 1. Which refers, directly or indirectly, to any testimonial of any kind concerning the investment adviser or concerning any advice, analysis, report or other service rendered by such investment adviser…."

In a release last year about social media, the commission added: "The term "testimonial" is not defined in Rule 206(4)-1(a)(1), but SEC staff consistently interprets that term to include a statement of a client's experience with, or endorsement of, an investment adviser."

SEC rules pertaining to advertising past performance are complex, and such communication should be reviewed in totality by compliance to ensure it is not misleading to any parties who may receive it.

Now that's out of the way, you've seen it's taken an incredible amount of time and effort to get where I am now.

PREFACE

Through more than fifteen years of tremendous effort and expense deciphering endless financial data, applying complicated mathematics, researching cryptic securities regulations, acquiring the necessary licenses, and putting up over a million dollars of my own money, I discovered how to use the secrets of investment banks and hedge funds the hard way.

Now, I can provide you the easy way.

If you've been struggling in the past, either with sustaining a profitable investment portfolio or raising capital to grow your investment business, it's not your fault. The system is designed to beat you.

I want to help you beat the system!

Here's a quick breakdown of what was required to accomplish just a couple of the key milestones on my journey:

<u>First Fund</u>

- $70,000 for offering documents (private placement memorandum, fund operating agreement, subscriptions docs) and entity formation
- $35,000 for marketing documents (data aggregation, summary, pitch book)
- $100,000 (minimum) to open an account with UBS
- $175,000 retainer for placement agent and administrator onboarding
- 3 years of prior successful investing experience
- 1 year of research into quantitative methods in finance

<u>Boutique Investment Banking Services</u>

- $1 million plus and 3 years developing operational and distribution infrastructure

- 11 years of developing broker-dealer and RIA relationships
- 6 years of research into securities law and banking history

I've broken out everything we're going to cover in this book into three shadow banking secrets:

Secret #1: How to meaningfully measure risk (quantitatively) to identify assets that will best perform across market cycles (including financial crises).

Secret #2: How to quickly grow your investment portfolio (AUM) to 9-figures and beyond.

Secret #3: How to be compliant as you quickly scale your investment business.

Almost every real estate syndicator operating outside the broker-dealer space that I talk to is breaking some securities law, and they don't even know it. Often, they've been doing it for years and don't find out until it's too late. When it finally does catch up with them, the outcome is usually tragic.

On the financial services front, nearly every broker-dealer due diligence officer ("DDO") we speak with recognizes the need to quantitatively measure the risk associated with the alternatives they consider hosting on their platform but have no means to do so. And stuck in the middle, seemingly every financial advisor has been conditioned to accept the notion that their clients' portfolios are fated to ride the inevitable peaks and valleys of the markets.

Collectively, these three secrets address all of the fundamental obstacles preventing everyone from financial professionals to retail investors from reaching their loftiest financial goals.

Secret #1
Engineering Risk-Adjusted Investment Performance

The secret skill that made top shadow banks over 20% during the 2008 financial crisis and every year since...

WHAT IS RISK?

It all starts with this fundamental question:

Most people unwittingly expose themselves to catastrophic risks. To effectively manage risk, you first must be able to define it. Do you know what risk actually means?

SECRET #1: ENGINEERING RISK-ADJUSTED INVESTMENT PERFORMANCE

Every investor—from the guy who bets on physical currency by hiding it under his mattress to Ray Dalio—is concerned with risk. Somewhat surprisingly, though, despite the fact that the vast majority of people are risk-averse, very few have any idea what risk actually means. This group includes the vast majority of financial professionals. And ironically, despite retail investors' often stated aversion to risk, they and their advisors tend to solely focus on the projected return of an investment, seldom (read: never) considering the risk associated with achieving the expected return in any meaningful way. Sure, most people take a look at a few qualitative variables that may contribute to an investment's risk, but this is tantamount to seeing flour on a random countertop and walking away confident you're going to get a delicious cake. Successful baking requires a specific recipe of precisely measured ingredients. It doesn't work if you only use a few of all of the ingredients required, eyeball the quantities, and make up a plausible story about what's going to come out. If this haphazard approach isn't good enough for baking, why is it good enough for you or your clients' life savings?

Before we can begin to discuss ways to manage risk effectively, we must first define it. Risk is quite simply the likelihood or probability of a negative event occurring weighed by the potential loss associated with such an event. In other words, it is a number that can be computed, and because financial assets are measured in quantifiable units such as dollars over time, so can the potential downside. The people who calculate these measures for investment banks and hedge funds are called quantitative analysts, or quants.

The following section of this book gets fairly technical, and it's very much okay if you don't follow all of the mathematical details. The takeaway from this section is that ***risk is a number***, and if you don't understand the quantitative techniques required to measure it accurately, you'd better find and work with someone who does (beyond the ability to simply parrot some vernacular and acronyms).

Risk probability is measured as the degree to which something changes. In finance, we're concerned with changes in market values, what is referred to as price volatility—the greater the volatility or change in the price of an asset, the riskier it is said to be. (It's worth noting that price and value can become disconnected. As Warren Buffet said, "Price is what you pay. Value is what you get." We'll touch on that a bit later.) The study of computing probabilities is the purview of the mathematical branches of statistics and probability theory, and herein lies the reason so few people understand risk.

People tend to dislike math. The human brain evolved to make quick, simple, intuitive judgments to avoid obvious threats such as venomous snakes and ravenous predators. There was (and for many people to this day still is) little need for mathematics in survival, and if anything, the intellectual resources required to use it would have been a waste of precious energy. Unfortunately, in finance, risks are not so obvious and require a considered approach to manage them effectively. In fact, they are extremely complicated and require not only a keen qualitative understanding of an investment's associated business factors but also correspondingly complex math to measure them in a meaningful way. It's worth emphasizing that computations alone are not enough. One of the most significant causes of the 2008 financial crisis was not the arithmetic, but a poor effort to identify the contributing variables to include in the calculations. It's arguable that these factors were deliberately omitted to maintain the highly profitable game of musical chairs for as long as possible, but that's another story.

So, in lieu of math, when most people consider risk, they revert to an intuitive feeling that most often bears little resemblance to reality. A fairly common example of this phenomenon is the person who is afraid to fly on a commercial plane but has no problem speeding through traffic on a congested highway where the probability of fatality is demonstrably higher. A significant contributing factor to this misestimation is the fact that people tend to believe that their control over a situation reduces risk, when often, especially in financial matters, the converse is true.

When it comes to investing, people's desire to reduce perceived risk through direct control is most often expressed through real estate investing, despite the fact that they know little to nothing of investing or real estate. A glaringly ironic example of this paradox is the ultra-high-net-worth individuals who rely on a family office for comprehensive investment and financial services except when it comes to real estate, where they invariably take the DIY approach. In the fairly rare instances when real estate investors begin to consider risk management, they tend to talk in operational heuristics: reduce risk by buying the worst house in the best neighborhood, using qualified professionals, borrowing on decent terms, etc. While these quasi-solutions begin to address issues that each contribute to the probability of a negative outcome, they fall short as was made painfully obvious by the colossal losses incurred by real estate investors in 2008. And just like pre-2008, lulled into a false sense of confidence by the bull market of the past decade, this round of DIY investors is not prepared for the next crisis that's likely to occur in the not-so-distant future.

So, memorize this and implement it into your investment decision-making process:

Risk is a number. It's the probability of loss weighted by the potential degree of that loss. Risk is not a feeling; it's not a relationship; it's not a story—it's a number.

That number is calculated with a bit of fairly complicated mathematics referred to as risk-adjusted performance measures. But that's just it, risk is something that can be measured, and the math behind it is just a complicated ruler that, when used properly, gives you an accurate measure of the quality of an investment or portfolio.

While most everyone is quite accustomed to thinking about investment returns in terms of percentages, risk should also be thought of as a percentage. Remember, it's the probability of loss weighted by the potential degree of that loss. Looking at an investment's potential return without taking into account its offsetting, measurable risk is like looking at the deposits in your checking account while ignoring the withdrawals. If you cannot measure the risk of investments—whether you're selling or you're buying—you're playing blind.

And that's the big secret. The mathematics of risk that govern financial loss with investments are just a more complex version of what governs the workings of a casino. The top brass of big financial firms uses that complexity to hide their insidious schemes through their captured and indoctrinated sales staff. But don't take my word for it, have a look at Greg Smith's book, *Why I Left Goldman Sachs*, which provides a candid look at the dynamics between the biggest financial firms and their clients. I particularly appreciate that he pointed out in his *60 Minutes* interview with Anderson Cooper that the skills required to construct and analyze such complexity are the domain of physicists, mathematicians, and engineers... not MBAs. Even the highly and rightly respected CFA designation does not confer sufficient mathematical skill.

Why I Left Goldman Sachs by Greg Smith.

Now, I'm going to arm you with these risk engineering skills, the same skills that we use in our third-party risk analytics and investment banking services, so that you can beat the big financial firms at their own game.

SMART VS. DUMB MONEY: ODD LOT THEORY

For those who still aren't convinced about the value of measuring risk and prefer to trust their feelings when it comes making investment decisions, I thought it would be valuable to share Wall Street's perspective on the market dynamic between emotional and mathematically skilled investors: the Odd Lot Theory as popularized by the bond statistician Garfield Drew in his 1941 book, *New Methods for Profit in the Stock Market*.

SECRET #1: ENGINEERING RISK-ADJUSTED INVESTMENT PERFORMANCE

In the pursuit to buy low and sell high, Wall Street views investors in one of two general categories: smart money and dumb money. Individual investors are dumb money. Smart money (good hedge-fund managers, private equity firms, etc.) reliably outperforms the market. Dumb money (individual investors, the sort of people who casually watch CNBC for stock tips) generally fares poorly. Individual investors are considered such dumb money that many professional investors regard them as contrary indicators (aka Odd Lot Theory): the lemming-like masses, often guided by their financial advisors, get excited and overly optimistic when the market's about to top, and they tend to get fearful and overly pessimistic when the market's about to bottom.

The result is that smart money continues to get richer, and dumb money continues to get poorer, especially around financial crises. This is why it is important for everyone to have a basic understanding of risk. By the end of this book, you will be smart money, if you aren't already.

After you peel away all of the licenses, professional credentials, and job titles, the degree to which an investor can answer this question is the degree to which he can be considered smart money: How do you evaluate risk?

The smart money is able to proactively manage risk, which ultimately allows it to maximize gains, limit losses, and inspire the confidence of others as a responsible steward of money.

The business of investing is the business of buying risk-adjusted returns at a good price.

That's worth re-emphasizing. The business of investing is not simply buying competitive expected returns from a respected brand; it's buying thoroughly measured risk-adjusted returns at a good price.

FINANCIAL CRISES

For risk-adjusted performance to be accurately measured, it has to take into account the effects of market crises. In other words, risk measures must encompass at least one complete market cycle worth of historical data. Otherwise, the extreme risk associated with financial crises goes completely unaccounted for. Granted, this analysis still won't tell you about the full effects of potentially greater crises than what we've experienced in the past or unforeseeable, unprecedented (black swan) events, but they give you a pretty accurate measure of how robust an investment is, especially for comparison purposes considering the scope and scale of 2008, from which we do have data for analysis.

Here's a sample of that data:

<u>2008 Financial Crisis</u>

- Dow Jones Industrial Average (DJI) fell from 14,164 on October 9, 2007 to 6,507 on March 9, 2009 for a 54% loss.
- Standard & Poor's 500 Index (S&P 500) fell from 1,565 on October 9, 2007 to 677 on March 9, 2009 for a 57% loss.
- Housing Price Index (HPI) fell from 185 on June 30, 2006 to 135 on December 31, 2011 for a 27% loss.

"September and October of 2008 was the worst financial crisis in global history, including the Great Depression."

BEN BERNANKE

Now, while the national average of actual losses in housing wasn't quite as bad as it felt in absolute terms, it was devastating considering the fact that if you had a mortgage with an LTV in excess of 70%, which was almost everyone who had recently

SECRET #1: ENGINEERING RISK-ADJUSTED INVESTMENT PERFORMANCE

purchased a house at that time, you lost your entire investment in that property, which accounted for a huge amount of most people's net worth, if not all of it.

Unfortunately, when people actually do begin to think about risk in meaningful terms, they tend to do so with a filtered or short-term memory. Almost everyone, including the financial advisor crowd, sweeps crises like that of 2008 under the rug as if everyone lost big, those losses were inevitable, and that they were a one-time event.

Financial crises would be bad enough if they were a once-in-a-lifetime event, but the reality is they're not. Here's a timeline representing the financial crises we've experienced over the past thirty to forty years. As you can see, they happen with some regularity—about once every ten years with a trend of ever-increasing magnitude, which means we're about due for another, and the fundamentals of the economy have been pointing to the next big one for a while.

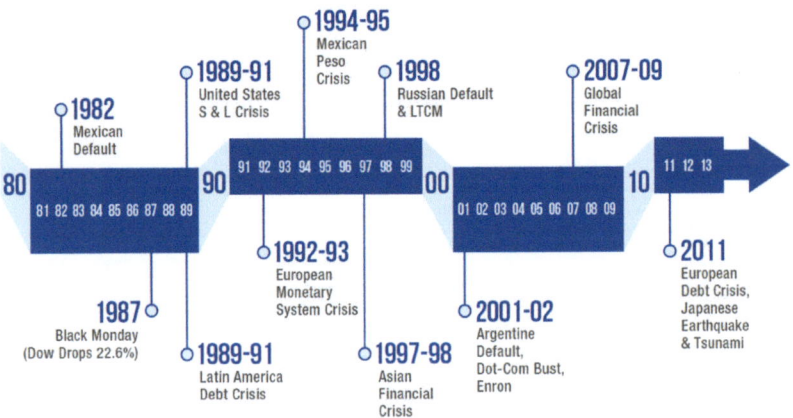

Financial crises tend to occur about once a decade with each one bigger than the last.

This brief history doesn't even include the skyrocketing interest rate environment that arose from Nixon closing the gold window on August 15, 1971, which led to the prime rate rising from 5.25% in December of 1971 to an almost unbelievable 21.50% on December 19, 1980.

Interest rates have been artificially suppressed by the Fed to hover around all-time lows for over a decade to mask the full effects of the 2008 crisis, which has forced the U.S. dollar between a rock and a hard place. The Federal Reserve, which is the prime issuer of the U.S. dollar, reported itself insolvent on a mark-to-market basis in its Combined Financial Report for Q3 2018. As we discussed in the prologue, the take-home story is that there is no way for this to end well. With the Fed having no ammunition left in its arsenal and an entire economy dependent upon cheap money, 2008 will look like a blip on the radar; it's just a matter of when.

The multi-trillion-dollar question is, "When will the next crisis occur, and what's the risk to you?"

The good news is that not everyone lost in 2008, or 1998, or 1989. A handful of people made out hugely profitable, and some of those same people have continued to do so during the bull market since. Isn't this a club you'd like to join?

The first step in joining that club is to understand how risk is measured.

AN INTRODUCTION TO RISK ANALYSIS IN NUMBERS—THE COIN FLIP

Here, we can begin to take a look at an intuitive example of risk as a number with the risk-adjusted performance calculation for the flip of a coin. I expect this simple example will drive the basic idea home very clearly.

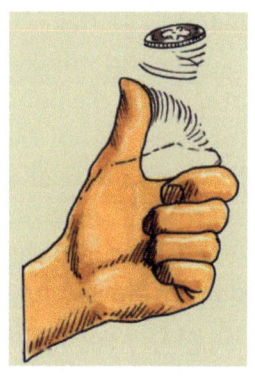

The risk associated with the outcome of a coin flip is the simplest to calculate.

With the flip of a coin, the probability of guessing which side will come up is one out of two, or 50%. If you were to put money on that outcome, what would be a fair return on that bet? The answer is double your money. For example, if you were to bet $1 on heads, a fair return for guessing correctly would be $2. In mathematics, the fair return would be expressed as $1 ÷ 50% = $2.

Under the simplest scenario, to determine the fair rate of compensation for a given risk, you simply divide the amount you plan to wager by the probability of achieving the desired outcome. If the output of that simple calculation is greater than what you plan to wager, then it's a good bet. Otherwise, it's not, as we'll see in the next example.

THE CASE OF THE TWO AND A HALF BILLION PERCENT RETURN

An extreme example of the concept of mispriced risk is that of a lottery ticket. The potential return on a $1 investment (i.e., purchase price) in the original Powerball yielded an average potential return of approximately $25,000,000 (the estimated average of Powerball jackpot cash payouts, not paid as an annuity) or 2,500,000,000%, but the risk of losing the total investment was approximately 99.99999943% (1:175,000,000 chance of winning).

This means that to make a $25,000,000 Powerball cash payout a fairly priced investment, a ticket should have cost approximately 14 cents ($25,000,000/175,000,000); the rest of that dollar, less operating expenses, became profit for the lottery corporation; the cash payout jackpot would have to have reached $175,000,000 before a $1 ticket became a fair bet.

Keep in mind these numbers don't take into account the risk of splitting the pot with another ticket holder, nor do they account for taxes. Again, the point of this example is to emphasize that a focus on potential return without adjusting for risk is a misguided approach to investing that leads most investors to overpay for assets.

This example highlights the glaring fault in how almost everyone thinks about investing. People, including most financial advisors, focus on fairly specific numbers to vet potential returns, but when it comes to evaluating the associated risk, which is the most important aspect of investing, a decent story or sufficient immediate compensation is all it takes to consummate a trade.

How can you possibly know if you're paying a fair price for an investment with this story-based approach to risk analysis?

The answer is that you can't. Who do you think benefits from you not knowing what you should be paying for your investments? I'll give you a hint; it's not you.

The good news is you can flip this script.

Not only is the probability of losing an important consideration to quantify in risk management, but it is even more important to consider the potential degree of that loss. In other words, what's the cost of losing versus the reward of winning?

THE SOLDIER'S BAD BET AND TAIL RISK

When evaluating risk, just as important as the probability of an outcome is the value of the positive outcome as compared to the value of the negative outcome. In mathematics, this idea is expressed as convexity, skewness, and kurtosis. The goal, in finance and life, is to make decisions that expose you to the greatest positive outcomes while risking as little as possible.

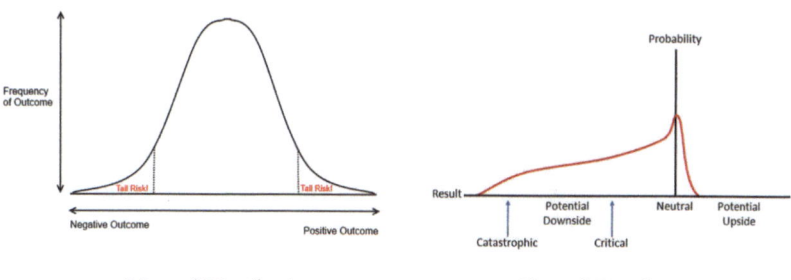

Normal Distribution   Skewed Distribution

Many young people are drawn to the promise of income and "free" education by the military in exchange for their service. While this may seem appealing as the positive outcome is guaranteed and the relative risk of being killed in action is low, the potential upside is limited (to a few tens of thousands of dollars in monetary value) while the potential downside is catastrophic (death). Although serving in the military is a noble pursuit, enlisting in the military is a very bad decision from a risk management perspective. In other words, the soldier's upside is finite, while his downside exposure is infinite.

SECRET #1: ENGINEERING RISK-ADJUSTED INVESTMENT PERFORMANCE

As a professional investor, you want to flip that dynamic. You want to pursue investments with infinite upside potential while being exposed to a finite downside and preferably a very small finite downside potential. In the world of investing, what type of financial instruments creates such an asymmetric, or positively skewed, risk-reward dynamic? I'll give you a hint—options—and we'll talk about them shortly.

But for now, suffice it to say that buying options creates positive convexity: small potential loss exposure with potentially infinite upside, and they can protect you from tail risk, which is described mathematically as kurtosis. I alluded to it previously when I referenced the recent history of financial crises. In simple terms, tail risk describes very low probability outcomes that occur more often than expected. Technically speaking, it's the risk of outcomes greater than three standard deviations from the mean occurring as depicted by the normal distribution, i.e., less than 0.3% of the time. The problems with tail risk are three-fold:

1. The normal distribution does not reflect reality, and tail risk tends to be fat-tailed, meaning that people have a short memory and dismiss events that occur about once every ten years or more as likely to never happen. In other words, people have a natural tendency to grossly underestimate the frequency of low-probability events.

2. Tail risk events are based upon things that you don't know that you don't know and are not accounted for in models that are solely predicated on past outcomes (especially when past data is limited to only a few years or less), which is another way of saying that the normal distribution is not an accurate model of reality. These unknown unknowns are what Nassim Taleb refers to as black swan events. The result is that most people get completely blind-sided by tail risk events, as was the case with the 2008 financial crisis.

3. As we just discussed, tail risk events can be catastrophic.

SOCIALIZATION OF RISK: THE FEDERAL RESERVE

The most insidious way in which the big box financial firms manage their risk exposure—allowing them to ignore their own risk analysis profitably—is through regulatory capture, which results in socialization of the very risk they create.

While many people look at the failures of banks and the 2008 financial crisis as evidence of big investment bank incompetence, they are missing a critically important piece of the puzzle. As we discussed in the prologue, the biggest investment banks are protected from loss by both the Federal Reserve (the Fed) and the federal government itself. The big banks' executives now know that if their firms make irresponsible investments, they get to keep their compensation without recourse, and their firm will be bailed out by the public, so their decisions are not based on ignorance, but rather a strategic understanding of their potential loss limits.

Everyone should be aware of how the big investment banks exploit the population, and no text addresses this subject better than *The Creature from Jekyll Island* by G. Edward Griffin.

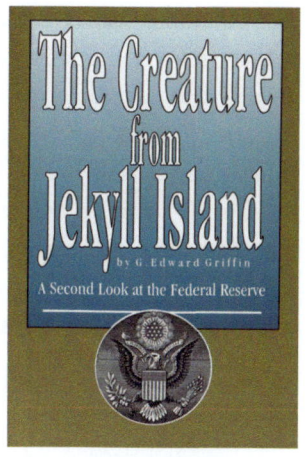

The Creature from Jekyll Island by G. Edward Griffin.

It's a must-read to understand the American economic and political telenovela that is courtesy of the big global financial interests.

Another type of measurable risk is the loss of investment return due to inflation, or inflation risk.

Arguably, the most poorly understood and insidious result of the banking cartel's influence over U.S. fiscal and monetary policy is inflation, or the loss of the purchasing power of a currency due to an increase in its supply. For example, if you grow $100 into $103 dollars over the course of a year, but items that cost $100 at the beginning of the year wind up costing $103 by the

SECRET #1: ENGINEERING RISK-ADJUSTED INVESTMENT PERFORMANCE

end of that year, your financial position has not really increased by the 3% that appears at face value. It's stayed the same in real terms as the increase in your amount of money is offset by an equivalent loss in its purchasing power.

It's generally accepted within the finance industry that the current nominal yield of the 10-year Treasury note represents the risk-free rate of return. The problem, however, is that the risk-free rate, after subtracting the inflation rate, is effectively zero. In other words, inflation completely eliminates the real yield of U.S. treasuries, and that doesn't even account for the fact that there actually is risk in holding U.S. bonds as fiscal and foreign policies threaten the stability of the U.S. dollar.

To make matters worse, the U.S. government's measure of inflation, the CPI, is generally manipulated to understate the actual rate of inflation (an honest analysis of economic data and inflation rates can be found at www.shadowstats.com), which makes the real yield of investments even lower, and in the case of the 10-year Treasury note, negative. In other words, you're actually *paying* the government to hold your money.

Peter Schiff of EuroPacific Capital once said he wished he could buy the CPI because of its eternally positive gains. Well, I'm going to show you, effectively, how to do just that.

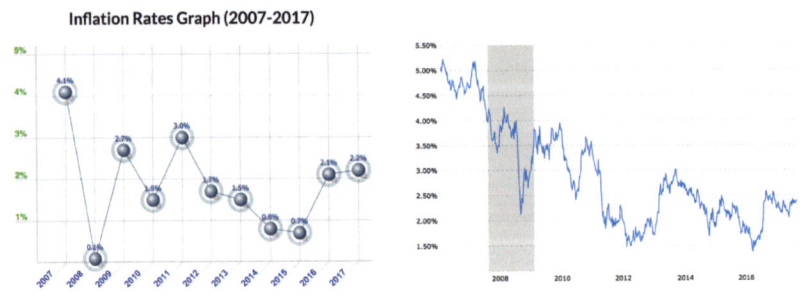

As of August 1, 2018

CPI (Trailing 12 Months): **2.95%**   10 Year Treasury: **2.96%**

The real yield of the 10-Year Treasury is effectively zero.

RISK-ADJUSTED PERFORMANCE MEASURES

Now, I'm going to introduce the most well-known, risk-adjusted performance measures of the religion that governs the financial services industry: Modern Portfolio Theory. I know this information is fairly dense, so it's okay if you don't follow the numbers, especially if you're a retail investor, but your financial advisor should be able to. The reality, however, is that you can pass all of the FINRA exams—the licensing exams for financial professionals—*without understanding these numbers*. As a result, many financial advisors don't have the skills to measure the risk of an asset or portfolio properly, and the CFA designation is no guaranteed remedy to this problem.

For this reason, it's important to at least briefly introduce the history, meaning, and calculations of the various risk-adjusted performance measures. And if you don't want to or are unable to do the math, I'll provide you the means to use these measures without having to.

Building on the earlier work of Harry Markowitz (who developed the idea of *beta* around 1952), the Capital Asset Pricing Model was independently introduced by Jack Treynor, William F. Sharpe (who also developed the Sharpe Ratio around that same time), John Lintner, and Jan Mossin between the years 1961 and 1966. Sharpe, Markowitz, and Merton Miller jointly received the 1990 Nobel Memorial Prize in Economics for this contribution. Michael Jensen took the next step in 1968 with his first use of *alpha*. The point of giving you this brief history is to highlight that these metrics have been around for a long time, and while they have some limitations, they have been recognized by the Nobel Foundation.

In finance, expected return (R_i) is equal to the geometric mean of an asset's, or a portfolio of assets', historical returns (not a guess about the future, i.e., pro forma). Risk is mathematically defined to be the measure of how much the price of an asset moves up and down, which is called volatility. Beta (β) compares the volatility of an asset to the volatility of the market: $\beta = 1$

SECRET #1: ENGINEERING RISK-ADJUSTED INVESTMENT PERFORMANCE

means the asset moves exactly with the market (usually defined as the S&P 500); a $\beta = -1$ means the asset moves in exactly the opposite direction of the market; $\beta = 0$ means the movement in the price of the asset has no correlation to the movement in the price of the market. The Capital Asset Pricing Model, or CAPM, is a statistical method used to measure volatility of an asset relative to the market and provides the fair risk-adjusted expected return $(E(R_i))$ as a percentage for an asset or portfolio given its risk characteristics. Alpha (α) is the additional return generated by an asset above what is fair as given by the CAPM; α is equal to R_i minus $E(R_i)$. The Sharpe Ratio (R_s) is a simpler risk-risk-adjusted performance measure that compares the total volatility of an asset to its expected return less the risk-free rate (R_f) (usually defined as the 10-year Treasury note); a Sharpe Ratio greater than 1 is considered good, greater than 2 is very good, and above 3 is excellent.

Beta	Geometric Mean	CAPM	Alpha	Sharpe Ratio
$\beta = \dfrac{Cov\left[\sum_{k=1}^{n} R_{i(k)},\, \sum_{k=1}^{n} R_{m(k)}\right]}{Var\left[\sum_{k=1}^{n} R_{m(k)}\right]}$	$\overline{R_\bullet} \equiv \left[\prod_{k=1}^{n}(R_{\bullet(k)}+1)\right]^{\frac{1}{n}} - 1$	$E(R_i) = R_f + \lvert \beta \rvert (\overline{R_m} - R_f)$	$\alpha = \overline{R_i} - E(R_i)$	$R_s = \dfrac{\overline{R_i} - R_f}{\sigma_i}$

Where: k = time interval; R_i = portfolio return; R_m = market return; R_f = risk-free rate of return; $E(R_i)$ = risk-adjusted expected return; σ_i = portfolio standard deviation

The most common risk-adjusted performance measures stated mathematically.

An understanding of the mechanics of these risk-adjusted performance measures has led the intellects of the industry to create additional measures that communicate different facets of risk, some of which go so far as to capture the very important third and fourth-order considerations: Treynor Ratio, Information Ratio, R-Squared, Modigliani Measure, Omega Ratio, Maximum Drawdown, and Return over Maximum Drawdown ("RoMaD"), Value at Risk, Monte Carlo Simulations, etc. I'm not going to dive into the math for each of these here—nor do I expect you really want me to—but it's important to know they exist and that each describe a different facet of risk. Some of these metrics, however, are more informative than others.

Here are the qualitative definitions of some of the more important risk-adjusted performance measures:

Liquidity-Adjusted Expected Return	Measures the break-even return of an investment given both its market risk and illiquidity. Only used for private or restricted securities.
Maximum Drawdown ("MDD")	Measures an investment's maximum loss from its peak to its trough before a new peak is attained. The lower the number, the better.
Modigliani Risk-Adjusted Performance ("M2" or "RAP")	Derived from the Sharpe Ratio, M2 measures the total risk-adjusted performance of an investment as a percentage. The higher the number, the better.
Omega Ratio (Ω)	Measures the total positive returns over the total negative returns of an investment. The higher the number, the better.
R-Squared	Measures the percentage of an investment's movement that can be explained by the market. R-squared of zero is ideal for actively managed portfolios.
Sortino Ratio	Identical to the Sharpe Ratio except that risk is defined to be only negative deviation as opposed to total deviation. The higher the number, the better.

It's worth noting that Return over Maximum Drawdown, or RoMaD, as the name implies, is simply Expected Return divided by Maximum Drawdown, or MDD.

SUMMERS ALTERNATIVE RISK RATING

Although *beta*, CAPM, *alpha*, and Sharpe are better known risk-adjusted performance measures, Modigliani, *omega*, and MDD are arguably the most informative. As a matter of fact, those are the three metrics we rely upon most. Here's why: MDD tells you what your potential downside is, which is a straightforward and fundamental thing to know; Modigliani captures both market risk and total risk as a second-order measure; and Omega captures all four statistical moments: mean, variance, skewness, and kurtosis. As a matter of fact, I've developed a matrix that

SECRET #1: ENGINEERING RISK-ADJUSTED INVESTMENT PERFORMANCE

takes all three of these metrics into account and provides one comprehensive, user-friendly risk rating: the Summers Alternative Risk Rating, or SARR:

	1	2 $f(M2, \Omega, E(Ri))$	3
A	A1	B1	C1
B $f(MDD)$	A2	B2	C2
C	A3	B3	C3

The Summers Alternative Risk Rating matrix.

The SARR matrix takes into account all four statistical moments (geometric mean, variance, skewness, and kurtosis) of both systematic and idiosyncratic risk, including total potential loss. The first index of the SARR matrix (rows A, B, and C) represents functions of Maximum Drawdown (MDD); the second index (columns 1, 2, and 3) represents functions of the Modigliani Measure (M2), Omega Ratio (Ω), and the asset's or portfolio's expected return ($E(R_i)$).

As you might be able to gather, A1 is the best rating possible, B2 is the break-even point, and C3 is the worst. I'm really proud of this matrix because it's the only rating ever created that captures all four statistical moments of risk with a single output, and it's not heavily dependent upon selecting the "correct" benchmark.

Stocks vs. Real Estate

Now that I've introduced the basics of risk-adjusted performance measures, let's start applying them, and what better place to start than to address the age-old debate over which market is better, real estate or stocks.

YEAR	S&P 500	MSCI US REIT
2004	10.88%	31.49%
2005	4.91%	12.13%
2006	15.79%	35.92%
2007	5.49%	-16.82%
2008	-37.00%	-37.97%
2009	26.46%	28.61%
2010	15.06%	28.48%
2011	2.11%	8.69%
2012	16.00%	17.77%
2013	32.39%	2.47%
2014	13.69%	30.38%
2015	1.38%	2.52%
2016	11.96%	8.60%
2017	21.83%	5.07%
2018	-4.38%	-4.57%

Annual returns of the S&P 500 and MSCI US REIT Indices from 2004 through 2018.

SECRET #1: ENGINEERING RISK-ADJUSTED INVESTMENT PERFORMANCE

Finally, here's the answer: the real estate market as represented by the MSCI US REIT Index, and the stock market as represented by the S&P 500. The data measured here goes back to 2004, which was the first year of the MSCI REIT Index. Note that the risk-free rate was taken as a snapshot of the 10-year T-note on January 15th, 2019 at 10:21:04 PM, EST.

MSCI US REIT CHARACTERISTICS

R_f	2.71%	Risk-Free Rate of Return (10 yr T-Note)	$\Sigma i-$	-91.70%	Sum of MSCI US REIT Annual Returns < E(Ri)
R_m	7.77%	Expected Market Return	$\sigma i-$	12.59%	Standard Deviation of MSCI US REIT Annual Returns < E(Ri)
R_i	8.20%	Expected MSCI US REIT Return	R_{so}	0.090	Sortino Ratio [(Ri - E(R0)) / σi-]
σi	20.13%	Standard Deviation of MSCI US REIT Annual Returns	Ω	1.510	Omega Ratio (Σi+ / -Σi-)
β	0.862	MSCI US REIT vs. S&P Covariance / S&P Variance	i_{max}	35.92%	MSCI US REIT Maximum Annual Return
$E(R_i)$	7.07%	Risk-Adjusted Expected MSCI US REIT Return [Rf + β * (Rm - Rf)]	i_{min}	-37.97%	MSCI US REIT Minimum Annual Return
α	1.13%	MSCI US REIT Excess Return to Risk Borne	MDD	48.40%	MSCI US REIT Maximum Drawdown
R_p	4.35%	MSCI US REIT Risk Premium [E(Ri) - Rf]	RoMaD	0.169	Return Over Maximum Drawdown [Ri / MDD]
R_e	5.49%	MSCI US REIT Excess Return to Risk Free Return [α + E(Ri) - Rf]	R_t	0.064	Treynor Ratio [(Ri - Rf) / β]
R_s	0.273	Sharpe Ratio [(Ri - Rf) / σi]	R_n	0.022	Information Ratio [Ri - Rm / σi]
σm	16.06%	Standard Deviation of the S&P's Annual Returns	ΣRie^2	30.02%	Sum of Regression Line Error Squared
M_2	7.09%	Modigliani Risk-Adjusted Performance [(Ri - Rf) * σm / σi + Rf]	ΣRie^2	57.34%	Sum of Error from Ri Squared
$\Sigma i+$	138.47%	Sum of MSCI US REIT Annual Returns > E(Ri)	R^2	47.64%	R-Squared (ΣRIe2 / ΣRle2)

S&P 500 CHARACTERISTICS

Rs = 0.315   Ω = 1.271   MDD = 37.00%   RoMaD = 0.210

Risk-adjusted performance characteristics of the S&P 500 and MSCI US REIT Indices.

SECRET #1: ENGINEERING RISK-ADJUSTED INVESTMENT PERFORMANCE

Take a minute to sift through all of these numbers, and see if you can identify which market is better, real estate or stocks and why. The takeaway here is that the markets are only marginally different. The opportunity for significant risk-adjusted performance lies with quality active management, not in aggregated secondary markets. Granted, good active managers can be very hard to come by, but they're the gold to be sought out.

As an aside, it's worth noting that third-party due diligence firms who know real estate want to see a minimum 300 basis point spread between cap rate and the average cost of debt as an indicator of the ability to perform.

TREND IDENTIFICATION

We just looked at the risk characteristics of two markets, but now we're going to take a look at one example of how innovative and skilled asset management can navigate trends and inefficiencies within markets to generate superior risk-adjusted performance.

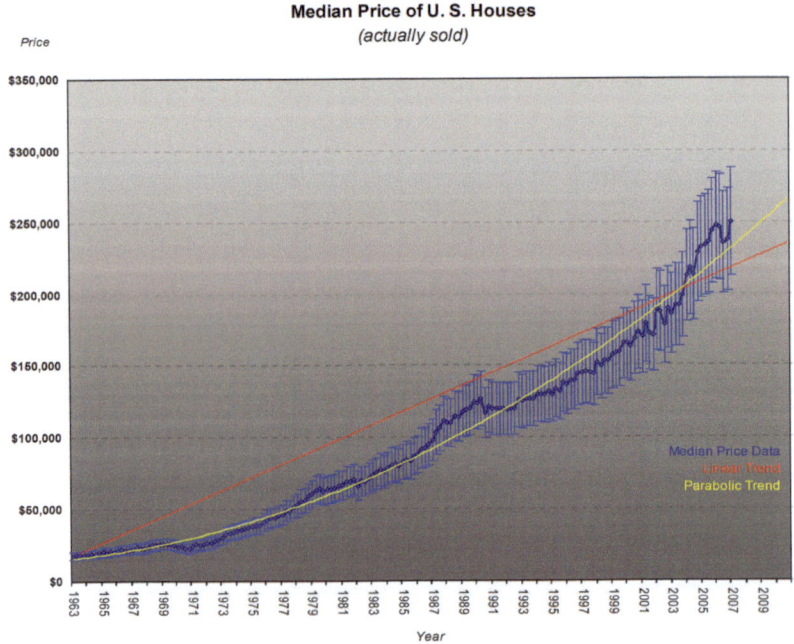

Linear and parabolic trendlines for the median price of U.S. houses from 1963 to 2007.

The graph captured here provides a fairly simple and clear illustration of how math properly applied to historical data can tell you a lot of very valuable information about the future that you'd otherwise have no way of seeing. I pulled this graph from an early 2007 draft of my ABL business plan. The data represented here by the blue, jagged curve is simply the median price of U.S. houses going back to 1963. I needed to use this data to make a prediction about future values.

As you can see, the blue line is not straight, but it's not a smooth upward sloping curve, either. One of the skills I had used quite a bit during my time in physics was determining which equation most accurately matched a given set of data. This is called interpolation. It's exactly the opposite of what you learned in high school algebra where you were given a formula and asked to graph it. Here, I've got the graph, and I needed to figure out the formula; that is what is represented in primitive form by the red line and yellow curve. The red line represents the linear formula that most closely matches the data (think $y = mx + b$), and the yellow line represents the parabolic formula (think $y = ax^2 + bx + c$). You can begin to see with this proto-iteration of interpolation the potential for how mathematical modeling can provide valuable insights about the future. Note that the actual linear trend I relied upon was a more complex function of market rent as you'll see in the next chart, but the point here is that I used this process of data analysis, interpolation and mathematical modeling to establish the maximum loan-to-value I was willing to lend through the ABL fund, which was admittedly conservative, and I'm glad it was.

Why is this important? Well, if the banking industry had performed this same mathematical exercise to guide their mortgage underwriting, we wouldn't have had a financial crisis in 2008.

RESIDENTIAL REAL ESTATE FUNDAMENTALS

Beyond confirming the validity and value of trend identification, the particular data sets graphed in the chart below begin to highlight the biggest advantage that non-traded alternative assets have

SECRET #1: ENGINEERING RISK-ADJUSTED INVESTMENT PERFORMANCE

over their traditional publicly-traded counterparts. The biggest problem in sticking with publicly-traded assets is the secondary market itself. It is efficient, which leads to a virtual zero-sum risk-reward dynamic, and it can move quickly and dramatically. Private alternative asset markets are very different.

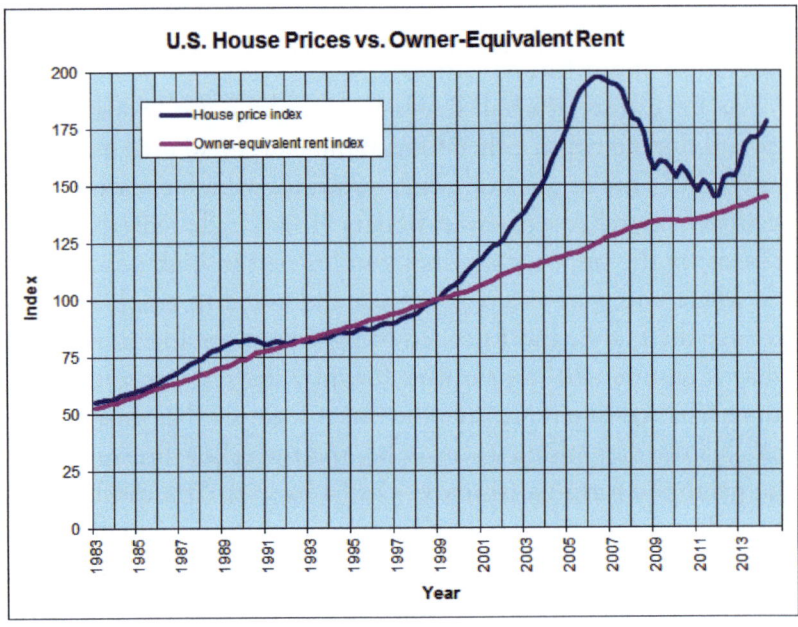

House Price Index and Owner Equivalent Rent from 1993 to 2014.

The graph here highlights the specific example we have been able to capitalize on, and in over 15 years, I've yet to see any other fundamental metric that provides the same systematic opportunity to generate risk-adjusted performance: residential rental income. While the residential rental market is affected by the economy at-large, it can be accurately evaluated based upon fundamentals to a much greater extent than the public equities markets. Even as manipulated interest rates and speculation have induced artificial housing prices, the rental market has remained relatively stable. As you can see, while comparable sales values represented here as the Housing Price Index ("HPI") have obviously bubbled, the income itself as represented by Owner-Equivalent Rent ("OER") glides along very similarly to the CPI.

What this chart shows—contrary to what most Realtors and appraisers are likely to proffer—from an investor's standpoint, is that it's important to value residential real estate as a function of its rental income as opposed to comparable sales. For an investor, a piece of residential property can and should be viewed analogously to a business.

For stocks, the approximate historical average price to earnings (P/E) ratio has been 16:1. This concept can be applied to residential markets as a means to determine stable value. A P/E ratio of 16:1 translates in real estate terms to a cap rate (annual net rent divided by value) of 6.25%. Each local market has its own historical average cap rates, and acquiring real estate assets, either debt or equity, with a basis that equates to the local historical maximum cap rate creates a very low-risk, high-yield investment.

As one might imagine, there is stiff competition for "good deals" in residential real estate as many large private funds such as those sponsored by Blackstone Group (NYSE: BX) have swept in to capitalize on this market. Such competition makes it increasingly difficult to find income-generating residential property at above historical average cap rates, but the advantages of owning real estate assets at the right price and under the right structures justify the effort. So, if you can't buy in your market at the right basis, become the lender.

The irony here is that residential real estate, and by extension multifamily, investors are a dime a dozen, yet almost all of them miss capitalizing on this dynamic. The tragedy and opportunity lie in the fact that they're all doing the same damn thing. From the biggest REITs to the smallest mom-and-pops, they tend to just buy at market value and hope for an eternally appreciating future. If you are acquiring real assets at market values or lending at a market LTV, you are subject to effectively the same market risks as any other asset class. But if you structure investment vehicles that are valued as a fixed, disciplined multiple of the income itself as opposed to market cap rates, then you have effectively created an asset that is better insulated from market risk than anything else available.

This can be achieved, as we did, by a de facto loan structure with a basis calculated as a fixed multiple of income as opposed to some arbitrary LTV. Further, various derivatives can be employed, such as swaps and options to extract the stability of the income and potential upside without substantial downside exposure. To make matters even better, because the real estate market is an inefficient, unsophisticated private alternative asset class, especially on the small balance side, there are substantial holes that create tremendous arbitrage opportunities that can be capitalized on by savvy asset managers, not only in terms of acquisition costs, but in terms of capital structure development and derivatives pricing. Nothing even close to this opportunity exists in the public capital markets.

While investment models built on residential income represent the greatest opportunity to generate unparalleled risk-adjusted performance, there are many other private alternative asset classes that provide similar opportunities. They tend to be a bit more complex and a little less prolific, but they're out there.

To help inspire confidence in their strategies, regardless of asset class, private fund managers can, should, and often do utilize third-party administration, provide quarterly reporting, and provide annual audits. This should help offset financial advisors' false sense of security in the "transparency" of public equities at the expense of real risk-adjusted performance opportunities. If they only knew how fabricated those corporate quarterly earnings reports really are (ask me how I know) or had any meaningful recollection to what extent that "transparency" protected them during the last financial crisis…

All that being said, the first step in overcoming the grossly limiting false belief that all alternatives are inherently riskier than stocks, bonds, and mutual funds is for financial market participants to begin thinking and communicating about risk in objective, quantitative terms.

It's worth noting that large pension funds, endowments, and other sophisticated institutions have already figured this out as they report alternative allocation to comprise between 30% to 60% plus of their total portfolios and have substantially outperformed the market for doing so. So, the next time you hear a retail financial advisor assuredly malign alternatives as if they are some sort of monolithic collective of high-risk, remember this fact.

DERIVATIVES—CONTROL THE RISK-ADJUSTED RETURNS OF ANY ASSET

Now, taking a look at the mechanics of how to capitalize on market inefficiencies, once you've identified a reliable trend or arbitrage opportunity, as I alluded to earlier, derivatives can be used to isolate and take advantage of it. A financial derivative is a contract that derives its value from the performance of an underlying asset. Basic derivatives contracts include swaps, futures, forwards, and options. While this book is meant to address alternative asset classes in general, real estate presents a tremendous opportunity for the utilization of derivatives.

Swaps

A swap is an agreement between two parties to exchange sequences of cash flows for a set period of time. Usually, at the time the contract is initiated, at least one of these series of cash flows is determined by a random or uncertain variable, such as an interest rate, foreign exchange rate, equity price or commodity price. Swaps do not trade on exchanges, and retail investors do not generally engage in swaps. Rather, swaps are over-the-counter contracts primarily between businesses or financial institutions that are customized to the needs of both parties.

Swaps in Real Estate

As an example, a swap in real estate can be created if one party is willing to trade the net operating income of a property, which can be variable, with a fixed interest payment on a commensurately valued note. The real property owner engaged in such a swap would be betting that the income from the property would be less than the income from the note, while the note owner would be betting the opposite. Swaps can be a great tool to bet against overly optimistic market participants.

Futures & Forwards

Both futures and forward contracts involve the agreement to buy and sell assets at a future date. Forward contracts do not trade on an exchange and settle at the end of the contract, while futures contracts do trade on an exchange and settle daily. Most importantly, futures contracts exist as standardized contracts that are not customized between counterparties, while forward contracts are customized between two parties to buy or sell an asset at a specified price on a future date.

Forwards in Real Estate

One simple example of a forward is a purchase contract on a house. If a house has a current market value of $500k, and the purchase contract has a sale price of $450k, then the purchase contract has a potential value of $50k. Of course, there are many considerations that affect the value of the purchase contract such as the method/accuracy of estimated market value of the underlying house, term (time left to close), transaction fees, and perceived strength of the buyer, but regardless, both in theory and in practice, the assignable real estate purchase contract is a derivative that can be sold (i.e., assigned) in the open market to another party for a fee.

Options

One of the most prolific and powerful financial derivatives is the option. There are two basic types of options: the call option, or call, and the put option, or put. A call is what is utilized in the traditional lease-option, which is familiar to most real estate professionals. The put, on the other hand, is virtually unheard of in the world or real estate.

An option, call or put, can be used as a standalone contract or in various combinations simultaneously to bet on any potential outcome. In other words, option strategies can be structured to profit from an asset rising in value, falling in value, not changing in value, or by its value moving in any direction, up or down.

Most importantly, options allow investors to create risk-return asymmetries, or positive convexity, exposing them to infinite upside with only a small finite downside.

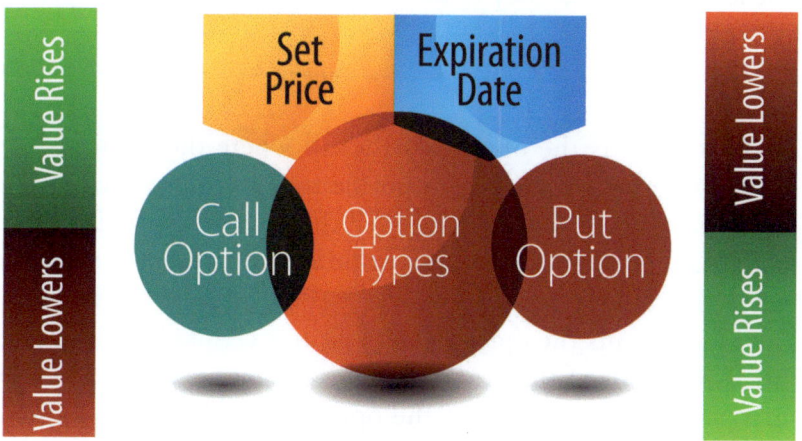

The anatomy of options.

Call Option

A call option is an agreement in which an investor pays someone else, a counterparty, for the right, but not the obligation, to buy something (i.e., underlying asset) at a specified price within a specific time period, or term. This payment is called an option fee, consideration, or premium. It may help to remember that a call option gives an investor the right to "call in" (buy) an asset. An investor profits on a call when the underlying asset increases in price. A call option is said to be in the money when the purchase price of the underlying asset, or strike price, is below the market price of the underlying asset (plus the option fee if it is not credited to the strike price); the call is out of the money when its strike price is above the market value (again, plus the option fee if it is not credited to the strike price).

In the case of the lease-option (which is two separate agreements: a lease and a call) investors are generally banking on either the underlying property appreciating during the term of the option or they believe they have negotiated a strike price that is below current market value with no expectation of the property falling in value, or depreciating, during the option term. It's worth noting that the lease is not necessary to benefit from the value of the option.

Put Option

A put option is the opposite of a call where the owner of an underlying asset pays an option fee to a counterparty for the right, but not the obligation, to sell the asset at a specified price within a specified time. A put option is said to be in the money when the strike price is above the market price of the underlying asset (minus the option fee if it is not credited to the strike price), and out of the money when its strike price is below the market price (again, minus the option fee if it is not credited to the strike price). A put becomes valuable as the price of the underlying asset falls, or depreciates, relative to the strike price.

For example in real estate, if an investor buys a put option on a property for $500k with a term of two years, he has the right to sell the house for $500k at any time during that two-year period to the counterparty of his put. An investor might do this if he thinks the market might crash during the put option term or if he believes he overpaid for the property. Put options can act as a form of insurance against a depreciating asset or crashing market.

Long and Short Option Positions

For both calls and puts, an investor can take either side of the contract, the long or the short position.

In the case of call options, a long position is the right to buy (call) the underlying asset. For the long call holder, the payoff is positive if the asset's price exceeds the strike price by more than the premium paid for the call. Short call holders believe an asset's price will decrease; they are said to sell, or write, a call. If an investor sells a call, holding a short position, he gives up control to the buyer of the call (the long call) who determines whether the option will be exercised. For the writer of the call, the payoff is equal to the premium received from the buyer of the call if the asset's price declines, but if the asset rises more than the strike price plus the premium, then the writer will lose money when the option is exercised.

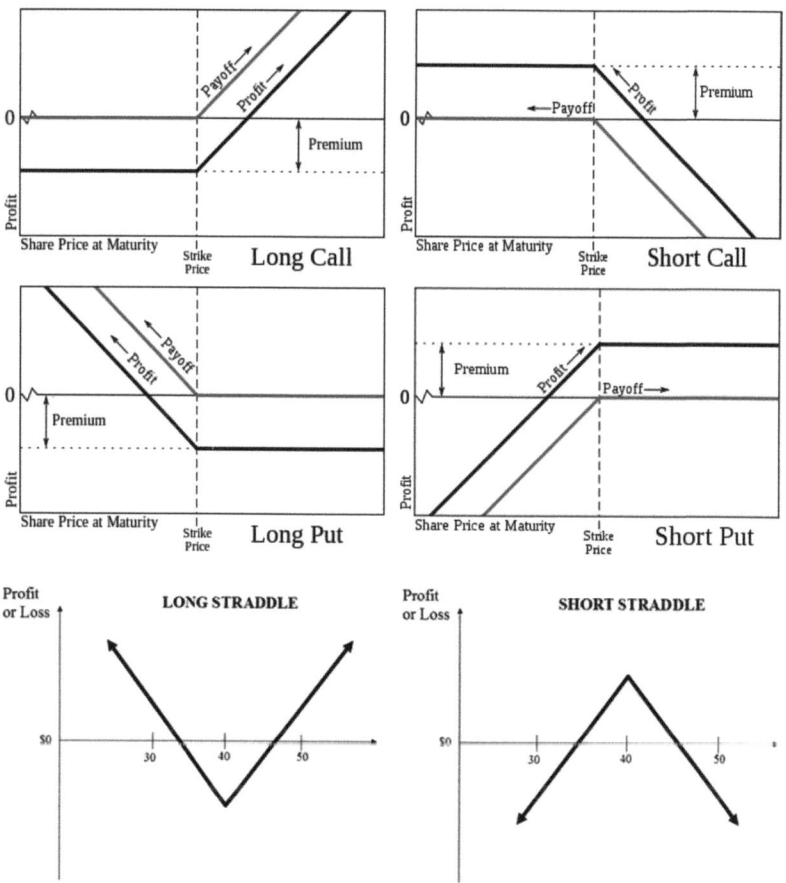

Option positions.

Like a short call position, long put holders believe an asset's price will decrease and buy the right (long) to sell (put) the underlying asset. For the long put holder, the payoff is positive if the asset's price is below the strike price by more than the premium paid for the put. Short put holders believe the asset's price will increase and sell or write a put. For the writer of the put, the payoff is equal to the premium received by the buyer of the put if the asset price rises, but if the asset price falls below the strike price minus the premium, then the writer will lose money when the option is exercised.

The Straddle and Other Simultaneous Options

While options can be used to generate returns based on an expectation that an asset's price will move in a particular direction, they can also be used to generate returns based upon an expectation of whether an asset's price will simply move at all (i.e., experience volatility). A straddle is an investment strategy involving the purchase or sale of a put and call option at the same time on a single asset with the same strike price and term; this allows the holder to profit based on how much the price of the underlying asset moves, regardless of the direction of price movement. The purchase of the call-put pair is known as a long straddle and profits are made from significant price movement up or down insofar as the price of the underlying asset increases or decreases more than the amount of the option fees paid. The sale of the put-call pair is known as a short straddle and profits are made from stagnant pricing as the owner of the short straddle collects option fees for both the put and the call when neither will be exercised. It is worth noting that options can be used in many various combinations to accomplish any number of hedging strategies.

Options in Real Estate

While option strategies are considered basic knowledge for financial professionals, they are hardly understood by real estate market participants, and herein lies a tremendous opportunity.

Option strategies represent a relatively inexpensive, low-risk approach to betting on any possible outcome an asset may experience; all that is needed is another party with the conviction to put their money up in support of the opposing view. Real estate brokers are perfectly positioned to carve out an enormous niche by matching such counterparties and to establish real estate derivatives as a liquid investment market. The potential for both transaction-based and consulting revenue is unlimited.

No one in the small balance (<$50 million) real estate market has any idea how to price an option. Think about the opportunity that creates. It is common practice for real estate owners to charge disproportionately small option fees for the right to buy their property at a given price (especially when a call is paired with a lease), which affords real estate investors the unique opportunity to recognize substantial upside potential while incurring very little risk. This disproportionate, or asymmetric, risk-reward profile (i.e., positive convexity) is the ultimate goal for professional investors.

For us, the application of options in real estate is not just theory; we built an entire fund on them. We were able to take advantage of informational and capital flow inefficiencies in the small-balance residential market with our asset-based lending, or ABL, model. We utilized a lease-back with an option structure in lieu of a traditional mortgage with valuations predicated on historical multiples of comparable rents to bet against comparable sales-based valuations. The result was that if our counterparty performed, we won. If our counterparty didn't perform, we won bigger, and the profitability of these trades had no dependence upon the phase of the market cycle.

QUANTITATIVE RISK MANAGEMENT APPLIED TO REAL ESTATE

Tying together everything we've talked about so far, this is what the performance of our asset-based lending model looked like as evaluated in quantitative risk-adjusted terms.

SECRET #1: ENGINEERING RISK-ADJUSTED INVESTMENT PERFORMANCE

Annual Returns

	ADAGIO ABL	S&P 500	MSCI US REIT
2007	26.32%	5.49%	-16.82%
2008	32.07%	-37.00%	-37.97%
2009	41.56%	26.46%	28.61%
2010	26.32%	15.06%	28.48%
2011	27.71%	2.11%	8.69%
2012	33.36%	16.00%	17.77%
2013	25.96%	32.39%	2.47%
2014	20.93%	13.69%	30.38%
2015	27.26%	1.38%	25.20%
Average *	**28.94%**	**6.40%**	**6.92%**

* Geometric Mean

Capital Asset Pricing Model ("CAPM")
$E(R_i) = R_f + |\beta|*(R_m - R_f)$

Sharpe Ratio
$R_s = (R_i - R_f) / \sigma$

ABL vs. S&P Covariance		S&P Variance
0.00017		0.03545

REIT vs. S&P Covariance		REIT Variance
0.02892		0.01086

Risk-Adjusted Performance Measures

ADAGIO ABL		
Rf	2.27%	Risk Free Return (10 yr T-Note as of 12/31/15)
Rm	6.40%	Expected Market Return (S&P Average Annual Return)
Ri	28.94%	Expected Asset Return (ABL Average Return)
σ	5.82%	Standard Deviation of ABL Annual Returns
β	0.0047	ABL vs. S&P Covariance / S&P Variance
E(Ri)	2.29%	Risk-Adjusted Expected ABL Return
α	26.65%	ABL Excess Return to Risk Borne (Ri - E(Ri))
Rp	0.02%	Asset Risk Premium (E(Ri) - Rf)
Re	26.67%	Asset Excess Return to Risk Free Return (α + E(Ri) - Rf)
Rs	**4.579**	**Sharpe Ratio**

MSCI US REIT		
Rf	2.27%	Risk Free Return (10 yr T-Note as of 12/31/15)
Rm	6.40%	Expected Market Return (S&P Average Annual Return)
Ri	6.92%	Expected Asset Return (REIT Average Return)
σ	21.55%	Standard Deviation of REIT Annual Returns
β	0.8159	REIT vs. S&P Covariance / S&P Variance
E(Ri)	5.64%	Risk-Adjusted Expected REIT Return
α	1.28%	REIT Excess Return to Risk Borne (Ri - E(Ri))
Rp	3.37%	Asset Risk Premium (E(Ri) - Rf)
Re	4.65%	Asset Excess Return to Risk Free Return (α + E(Ri) - Rf)
Rs	**0.216**	**Sharpe Ratio**

Risk-adjusted performance characteristics of Adagio's ABL strategy.

While many people, including most financial professionals, may require a bit of a learning curve to fully grasp the meaning of these numbers, the fundamental fact remains that audited quantitative measures of performance over a minimum of one complete market cycle are the only meaningful criteria by which to evaluate the quality of any investment, and by extension, any portfolio or asset manager.

While many hedge funds use these measures, they typically do so with a relatively short period of performance data. Without performance data that spans a minimum of one complete market cycle, the output paints a grossly incomplete picture, which is why I think more of the better financial advisors don't incorporate such metrics into their business. There just aren't enough players using sufficient quality performance data to make it a meaningful comparison tool.

That being said, if your asset management or investment business is actually better than what is otherwise available, and you want to successfully compete with the glut of mediocre traditional assets and advisors littered across the landscape, this is how you do it. You communicate your performance in these well-established quantitative terms with a minimum of one complete market cycle of audited performance data. If you can do that, there is no reasonable argument anyone can make for not allocating patient capital to your asset management business.

The only other meaningful variable we haven't touched on yet is liquidity, but that's a played out excuse for not allocating to private alternatives that is grossly overused, especially in the case of private, fixed-income products and private equity for younger investors.

As a matter of fact, liquidity is one of the biggest justifications most financial advisors cite when objecting to private securities; yet on the flip side, they advise their clients not to touch their indexed, "liquid" portfolio for years (the liquid portion of the portfolio is allocated to money markets). What good is the liquidity of equities when short-term volatility has no regard for your long-term savings and retirement plans?

We fully recognize the need for liquidity and its role in a portfolio. We also recognize that maintaining an arbitrary 90% minimum of a portfolio in public securities is senseless and counterproductive, especially if the performance of the private alternatives exceeds the public options on both a liquidity and risk-adjusted basis.

BENEFITS OF QUANTITATIVE RISK ANALYSIS

To highlight the value of the meaningful application of quantitative analysis to private alternative assets, Mark Renz of Socius Family Office described it as a:

"A unique opportunity to effectively manage risk."

MARK RENZ, CFA, Chief Investment Officer, Socius Family Office

Mark runs one of the best family offices, if not the best family office, I've known. He takes his fiduciary responsibility as seriously as anyone. He has both the credentials of a CFA and the wisdom to translate his rare level of expertise into faithfully carrying out his fiduciary role without regard for the incessant corrupt forces of the industry to do otherwise.

In short, the skills of meaningful quantitative risk-adjusted performance analysis represent an absolutely unique opportunity for private alternative asset managers to enter the high-stakes game of institutional finance—especially with those institutions who are motivated by merit—and institutional finance is where the real money changes hands.

Due Diligence Officers

How much better will you be able to not only protect your firm, but support your reps with an accurate measure of the risk characteristics of the sponsors you vet and ultimately accept onto your platform?

Translating the numbers into tangible examples: a byproduct of comprehensive quantitative risk analysis is that the process identifies which sponsors are able to execute their strategy and liquidation schedule without cutting distributions. How would that ability improve your value to the market and protect you from liability?

Now you're probably thinking most sponsors don't have a track record that encompasses a complete market cycle. That's true, but rigorously constructing a theoretical track based upon all relevant, actual, accessible historical market data is the solution. You first must translate their investment model into a comprehensive set of rules, then identify every variable reasonable that contributes to their performance based upon those rules. From there, it's just a matter of researching and plugging in the actual historical data into those variables. Don't get me wrong, it takes a thorough understanding of statistical mechanics to create a meaningful theoretical track record, but the value of having it far outweighs the cost of not.

Third-Party Due Diligence Firms

How much more meaningful do your third-party due diligence reports become when you start quantitatively measuring the risk of sponsor offerings and providing an objective measure of their performance expectations? How much more valuable do you become—not only to the broker-dealer community but also to the RIA space—by meeting their needs as an outsourced due diligence service provider?

From a revenue perspective, how would your business model improve if instead of only being compensated on the front end of client engagements, you were able to establish an ongoing revenue stream measuring their risk-adjusted performance on an annual basis?

Again, how would your position in the industry improve if you were able to provide an accurate estimate of the risk associated with any alternative? We already have an example of what this can do for a firm via traditional assets with Morningstar.

RIAs

How valuable would it be to your business if you could clearly and confidently identify quality, low-risk alternatives that meet your clients' objectives in ways not possible with any boilerplate allocation to public equities, bonds, and mutual funds?

How would it help you grow your business and recruit new clients if you were able to measure and communicate the risk-adjusted performance of your portfolios?

Approximately 14 out of 15 RIAs do not recommend alternatives because of their perception of risk, opacity, illiquidity, and E&O considerations. While most are indeed bad investments, the best alternatives generate far better uncorrelated and absolute risk-adjusted performance than any traditional asset and provide transparent quarterly reporting in addition to annual audits. How would your business improve if you could confidently identify and access those gems?

Family Offices

How can you achieve responsible growth and capital preservation (especially across down cycles and market crises) if you haven't measured an asset's or asset manager's sensitivity to the market across at least one previous complete market cycle?

How do you know which asset managers are able to provide you the best opportunities for growth if you don't measure the risk that corresponds with that expected growth? Trendy investments do not equal sound investments, and AUM is not inversely proportional to risk.

Researchers from Purdue and Loyola Marymount conducted a study to evaluate *Size, Age, and the Performance Life Cycle of Hedge Funds*. They analyzed Lipper TASS and HFR monthly performance data ranging from January 1994 to December 2016, breaking it down into three groups: less than $10 million under management (small), $10 million to $100 million (medium), and more than $100 million (large). The results in short: the smaller the hedge fund, the more likely it is to outperform. As far as big funds are concerned: the younger they are, the better.

This is just one more example of how the heuristics and beliefs that govern institutional investors' allocation decisions are often misleading. What other false beliefs do you have that might be adversely affecting your investment decisions? The ability to acquire vast amounts of information from an ivory tower is not tantamount to effectively and objectively analyzing it.

Sponsors/Syndicators/Fund Managers (Firms Raising Capital)

How much more money would you be able to raise—how many more selling agreements, RIA, and qualified purchaser relationships, etc.—if you were able to measure and communicate the merits of your investment model in meaningful, quantitative terms that allowed you to be compared apples-to-apples with any other investment product in the market, from Apple stock to an index of student housing REITs?

For those newer sponsors that don't have a significant track record (or any track record at all, for that matter) how valuable would it be for you to be able to construct a theoretical track record that was recognized and respected by the industry for the objectivity and rigor that went into creating it?

Retail Investors

You're not expected to be able to calculate the risk measurements of investments. That being said, you have to know what risk is and

SECRET #1: ENGINEERING RISK-ADJUSTED INVESTMENT PERFORMANCE

what it's not. Risk is not a story; it's not a relationship; it's not a feeling. Risk is a number. It's the probability of loss weighted by the potential degree of that loss. If your financial advisor can't tell you the risk measures of an asset or portfolio, then you need a new financial advisor.

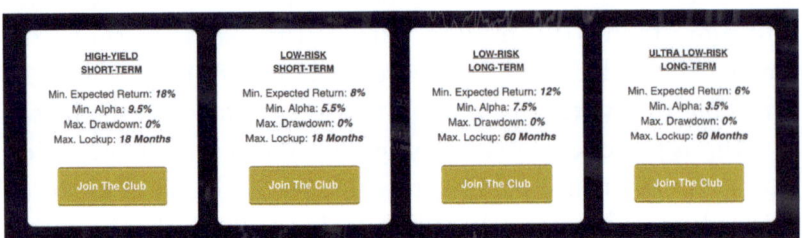

Investment clubs organized by appetite for risk, return and liquidity.

I know the vast majority of financial advisors are not great. Most broker-dealers are just looking to collect a commission on the next trade without getting pinched by the regulators, and RIAs are too preoccupied with client recruitment and minimizing liability to create any uniquely valuable solutions for you. That being said, there are a handful of very good financial professionals operating in the market who are willing and able to provide far more value than what they take in fees.

There's a large contingent of investors whose experience with financial advisors, stocks, bonds, and mutual funds has driven them to exit the markets and buy physical assets directly—most often, real estate. They tend to think direct ownership of physical assets equates to a risk guarantee. As we discussed earlier, the feeling of security afforded by the DIY approach is a mirage. The idea that a non-professional asset manager can navigate all of the pitfalls of managing a portfolio of assets, not to mention the infinitely complex dynamics of the market, is a fool's errand. Deciding the appropriate leverage ratios, identifying the phase of the market cycle, accounting for the variability in rehabilitation costs and timeframes, planning for the effects of vacancy, tax considerations… the list goes on and on. In short, control creates a blinding illusion that causes people to grossly neglect the risks they subject themselves to. Sure, some DIY investors may do well for a while when the market is heating up, but when the market comes back down, as we saw in 2008, the DIY crowd gets wrecked. Unless you plan to make asset management your career, you're best served to spend that effort finding one of the few really good alternative financial professionals already operating in the market.

SECRET #1 SUMMARY

To summarize and restate this extremely esoteric and invaluable first secret:

> "Risk is a number. It's the probability of loss weighted by the potential degree of that loss. As with anything else, if you want to manage risk effectively, you first have to measure it."
>
> BENJAMIN D. SUMMERS

A successful application of this fact is quantitative risk-adjusted performance analysis as measured across a minimum of one complete market cycle and applied to private alternative assets, specifically relying on well-designed capital structure and derivatives within inefficient markets such as small-balance residential income. Again, there are other very good private alternatives that provide the potential for similar risk-adjusted performance as underlying assets.

You're probably thinking this is way too complicated for you to deal with, or that you're not good at math so you won't be able to develop these skills, right? Well, I've got a couple solutions that will take care of all of the mathematics for you.

Secret #2
Creating Capital

The shadow banking secret to creating the exact amount of capital you need for your investment portfolio or business out of thin air...

PRIVATE SECURITIES ISSUANCE & THE SAVINGS CRISIS

Now that we've covered the first secret that deals with how to generate, analyze, and report performance that is measurably good enough to responsibly offer as a competitive investment, we now have to create the means for others to participate, or invest, in our asset management business, which leads to Secret #2:

> *By responsibly issuing your own private securities, you can raise tremendous amounts of capital both as debt and equity. Meanwhile, you will provide retail investors the means they desperately seek to grow their savings safely and generate retirement income.*

This is where the rubber meets the road.

As I think some of you already know, the 2008 financial crisis could have and should have been much worse than it actually was. Decades of irresponsible U.S. fiscal and monetary policies had built up enormous imbalances in the economy that needed to be corrected to make sure that the resources of the country are being utilized in ways that maximize the efficiency of people's work and provides the highest standard of living for all. That correction was never allowed to take place. As soon as the first rapid and dramatic wave of economic correction hit Wall Street, both Congress—and to a much greater extent, the Federal Reserve—injected trillions of freshly created dollars into the global banking system to stave off the imminent collapse. The result, while minimizing the immediate effects of the crisis, has created even further fundamental economic instability, which has the world primed for an even bigger collapse.

My research into this dynamic peaked around 2012 when the Fed was going all out with quantitative easing, which is just a sophisticated moniker for creating new money. Through that effort, I uncovered the most fundamental and profound levels of corruption you could imagine. As I mentioned earlier, there is no better work on this subject than G. Edward Griffin's *The Creature from Jekyll Island*. The good news is that my research also revealed the fine points of how to use the mechanics of money creation for good.

The ability to issue private securities is only one step removed from the process by which the Fed and commercial banking system create and multiply the money supply. The ability to create securities is literally the ability to create a form of money out of thin air.

You're probably thinking that of course people value the money and assets created by banks, but you're not a bank, right? Well, not yet, but I just showed you the esoteric risk-engineering skills the most sophisticated financial institutions use to give value to their products. Now, I'm going to show you how to convert those skills into valuable, salable assets that *you* can create out of thin air. When you create securities for sale that meet investors' demand for risk-adjusted returns and liquidity, the purchaser recognizes the value of the purchase price as part of their savings, and you have the equivalent amount of cash in hand to operate your asset management business. When properly managed, both the value of their securities and the value of your asset management business grow in tandem. By the time we're done here, you can be your own bank, if that's what you'd like to be. We'll show you how to create valuable capital at scale and escape your serf status under the banking system by employing its esoteric capital formation tools.

The ability to create better private capital than what's available in the public markets solves both sides of the problem highlighted here: one in three Americans has $0 saved for retirement.

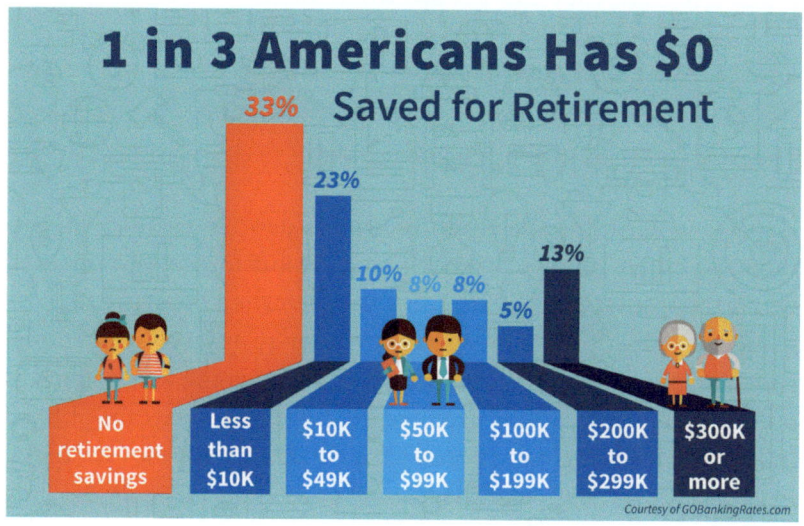

Americans' retirement savings.

Only 13% of Americans have $300,0000 or more saved for retirement. It generally takes at least $2 million to retire comfortably, and over 20% of the U.S. population is comprised of baby boomers; so that means most don't have anywhere close to what they need to retire, much less to retire in comfort. One of the many bad results of this statistic is that even those who do retire with a decent nest egg are forced to buy high-risk assets to achieve returns that are anywhere close to what they need to live on.

The ability to create quality private capital allows you to convert exclusive, valuable know-how into money more quickly and at a greater scale than what is afforded by any other business model, financial trick, or tip. You'll be able to create whatever value you want for yourself as retirement savings. In other words, if you don't see a way to save your way to retirement, the solution is to learn how to *create* the money you need for retirement—or anything else you'd like in life.

In the process, you'll gain the ability to serve those who do have retirement savings better than the dysfunctional institutions they currently rely upon by providing them higher returns with lower risk than they can get anywhere else.

Let's dive into the nitty-gritty of capital formation with a quick look at capital structure.

CAPITAL STRUCTURE

Capital structure is the combination of debt and equity instruments used to finance assets, including businesses. In general, when these instruments are sold, they're called securities.

When most people need money, they think in terms of borrowing. In capital markets terms, borrowing is the act of issuing/selling debt or notes that promise the purchaser a stream of fixed income. But debt (e.g., bonds) isn't the only type of financial instrument that can be issued.

Equity, or ownership interests (e.g., stocks), can also be sold, which affords the buyer participation in an asset's profits. In overly simplistic terms, equity can be thought of as the down payment above the debt required to buy an asset. People are generally aware of public equities, or stocks, such as shares in Apple, Inc. (NASDAQ: AAPL) or Exxon Mobil (NYSE: XOM), but private companies can also sell shares in their ownership to raise money. A common example is real estate syndication interests sold over crowdfunding sites.

One obvious point pertaining to securities issuance is that securities laws are complex. Most syndicators are aware that issuing equity represents a securities transaction, but what most don't realize is that debt, by default, is also a security. It's important to note that traditional bank borrowing represents an exception to the definition of securities issuance. If you're borrowing from the public, especially in the form of fractionalized notes or with the intent to use that money to generate a profit, you're almost certainly issuing debt securities.

CAPITAL STRUCTURE

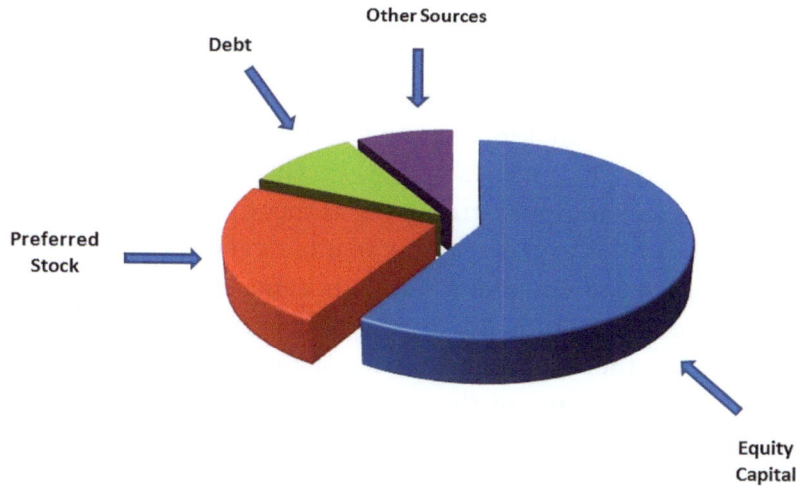

Components of capital structure.

The idea of capital structure is extremely important as the relationship between debt and equity not only profoundly affects the risk characteristics of your business, but it also goes a long way in determining the marketability of the securities you seek to issue.

For example, if your business is exclusively financed by debt that obligates you to 15% annual interest payments and your business only generates 12% per year in profit, you'll bankrupt yourself solely by virtue of having a poorly constructed capital stack. On the flip side—all else being equal—if your business was entirely financed by equity, you'd be fine.

The question becomes, *"What is the best ratio between debt, equity, and hybrids such as convertible bonds and preferred equity that maximizes profitability while minimizing risk?"* The answer is generally different for every business, given its specific characteristics. Having the ability to determine that answer is arguably half the battle in creating quality private capital.

It is fairly common for real estate syndicators to unwittingly run into trouble building the capital structure for their acquisitions. This is largely because they have been conditioned to take a passive role in the process. The percentage down payment required for a real estate acquisition, i.e., the percentage of equity, is typically dictated by the mortgage lender as a condition for writing a loan, and the borrower just goes along for the ride.

In this case, the borrower is relying on the bank to determine the capital structure for them, and often the terms of the down payment and debt can kill a deal. As we saw in 2008, banks aren't nearly as good at capital structuring as they'd like you to believe. Many of the mortgage-qualifying standards and restrictions they have in place are misguided and do nothing more than making the process more difficult for the borrower; they do little to nothing for the risk characteristics of the loan. (In your local bank's defense, many of these mortgage restrictions are passed down from the ivory tower of federal regulators.) When you're able to issue your own securities, you reap both the responsibility and the benefits of determining your business's capital structure.

Instead of a bank offering its savings account and CD depositors around 1% on their money to turn around and lend to you at 6%, if your business is sufficiently structured (taking into account cash flows, risk, etc.), you can cut out the middle man and offer would-be bank depositors 5 to 10 times what they'd otherwise get on their money without exposing them to additional risk while getting the capital you need on your terms.

To sell the securities you create, it's critically important that you understand the markets in which they are bought and sold. Keeping abreast of what's happening in the capital markets will tell you what types of financial products and what performance standards are in demand. This information should help guide you in the development of your capital structure.

CAPITAL MARKETS

What exactly are capital markets? Capital markets are the result of supply and demand where securities that are held for a minimum of one year are bought and sold (generally through intermediaries called broker-dealers). Markets include mechanisms to determine the price of traded assets, communicate price information, facilitate transactions, and effect distribution.

As a result of the Fed's monetary policy, there is approximately $20 trillion held in savings by U.S. workers who are in demand of decent low-risk real yield that is unmet by traditional financial assets. This creates a tremendous opportunity for private securities issuers to meet that demand.

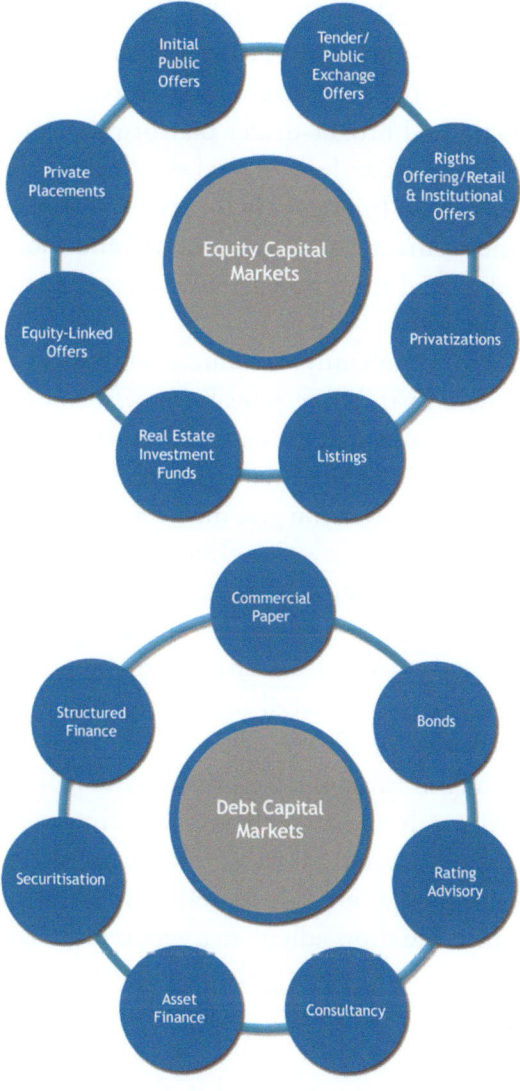

Capital markets.

To successfully create capital, you must strive to create better financial products on both a *risk* and *liquidity*-adjusted basis than what's otherwise available and bring them to the capital markets so you can outcompete the likes of Apple stock, U.S. Treasuries, and the litany of mutual funds being peddled by know-nothing sales guys.

It's worth noting that there are alternatives to broker-dealers in facilitating capital markets, but you have to be extremely diligent about not violating securities laws when utilizing these other means.

Have you ever tried to raise money outside the confines of bank borrowing and broker-dealer platforms? I've worked with quite a few clients who've done so, and every one of them who was raising money at scale (particularly for real estate) was unwittingly breaking some securities law or regulation, and more often than not, they had a hard time staying solvent as they grew without continuous corralling.

The goal is to compliantly structure your business in a way that makes you a demonstrably responsible steward of other people's money and to scale through the capital markets by creating better financial products. That's the name of the game as opposed to, "Hey, neighbor doctor, will you give me $100k for my syndication?"

As most people are aware, financial advisors—whether broker-dealer reps, Registered Investment Advisers or hybrids—are the gatekeepers to the public for the financial services industry. To maximize the potential for any public or private securities offering to fully reach the retail market, financial advisors need to be recruited into the distribution effort. Thanks to a history of incompetent and irresponsible private asset managers pushing deals that ultimately didn't perform, this can be more difficult than it sometimes should be for the few alternative asset managers and sponsors that are able to deliver superior performance.

Most financial advisors adhere to a very traditional asset allocation model built entirely upon publicly-traded securities. Outside of the fact that a set of relatively vague, qualitative criteria govern the literal value of their clients' life work, the substance upon which those models are predicated is a set of assets completely dependent upon schizophrenic secondary markets.

What's more remarkable is that the gross limitations of what effectively boils down to the sales function for a pump and dump business model are on full display in all of the FINRA texts, albeit in polished vernacular as a de facto disclaimer: *market risk is undiversifiable.*

TRADITIONAL PORTFOLIOS

To give you an idea about what you're competing against in the capital markets from a performance perspective, here's a sample of traditional portfolios made up of publicly-traded stocks, bonds, mutual funds, and money market instruments. The vast majority of financial advisors are driven by regulatory and revenue considerations to take a very generic, cookie-cutter approach to portfolio construction that includes just a few basic options. This is about as good as it gets when you go to your financial advisor and have him construct an investment portfolio for you based upon your "individual" risk appetite and growth needs—pick a box:

Sample Traditional Investment Portfolio Performance

	Conservative	Balanced	Growth	Aggressive growth
Annual return %				
Average	5.96	7.91	8.88	9.55
Worst one-year return	−17.67	−40.64	−52.92	−60.78
Best one-year return	31.06	76.57	109.55	136.07
Worst 20-year return	2.92	3.43	3.10	2.66
Best 20-year return	10.98	13.83	15.34	16.49
Historical volatility	4.52	9.61	13.13	15.83

Pie chart allocations:
- Conservative: U.S. stock 14%, Foreign stock 6%, Bond 50%, Short-term investments 30%
- Balanced: U.S. stock 35%, Foreign stock 15%, Bond 40%, Short-term investments 10%
- Growth: U.S. stock 49%, Foreign stock 21%, Bond 25%, Short-term investments 5%
- Aggressive growth: U.S. stock 60%, Foreign stock 25%, Bond 15%

Data source: Morningstar Inc., 2016 (1926–2016) courtesy of Fidelity Brokerage Services LLC The purpose of the target asset mixes is to show how target asset mixes may be created with different risk and return characteristics to help meet a participant's goals. You should choose your own investments based on your particular objectives and situation.

As you can see, the "conservative" portfolio lost almost 20% in its most down year. How can that possibly be deemed safe by any standard! Aggressive growth averages sub 10%? You can lend on conservatively valued real estate with a 35% equity cushion and do better than that—without taking a big hit in the down years.

No matter how you slice it, the results of traditional portfolio construction are not awesome, and that's due in no small part to the way in which financial advisors' are paid. Broker-dealers collect a commission on the sale of financial products, and Registered Investment Advisers ("RIA"s) get paid as a percentage of their total assets under management via the recruitment of high-net-worth clients. In neither case are financial advisors incentivized by the merits of their advice. As a matter of fact, they are very much *dis*incentivized by regulatory risk to do anything other than construct portfolios that conform to this very uninspiring template.

To make matters worse, between broker-dealers and RIAs, only RIAs have a fiduciary obligation to act in their clients' best interests, and even that does not equate to making a rigorous effort to assemble the best portfolio of investments possible. Many RIA firms delegate the actual construction of investment portfolios to what's called a turnkey asset management platform, or TAMP. You can imagine how valued the investment decision-making process is when it's delegated to a third party, and the results follow as you might expect.

If you can demonstrate organizational integrity, transparency, and performance that substantially exceeds this fairly low bar and addresses the regulatory concerns of financial advisors, what kind of opportunities do you think might exist for you to capture a piece of the tens of trillions of dollars of investable assets starved for low-risk fixed income and quality risk-adjusted growth?

For those of you who are financial advisors that recognize the shortcomings of the industry, wouldn't it be great to be able to provide your clients with products that are demonstrably better than what your competitors are able to offer?

PRIVATE INVESTMENT COMPANIES

Shares of equity in private businesses are not available for public purchase as is the stock of a publicly-traded company such as Apple Inc. (NASDAQ: AAPL). In general, publicly-traded companies must register with the Securities and Exchange Commission ("SEC") under the Securities Act of 1933; investment companies must also register under the Investment Company Act of 1940. A major type of company not covered under the Investment Company Act is the private investment company, which is simply a private company that makes investments but is exempt from registration with the SEC under Regulation D ("Reg D") of the Securities Act of 1933 and section 3(c) of the Investment Company Act of 1940.

There are a few different types of private investment companies, and they all fall under the category of alternative assets:

- Hedge Funds (open-end)
- Private Equity (closed-end)
- Venture Capital

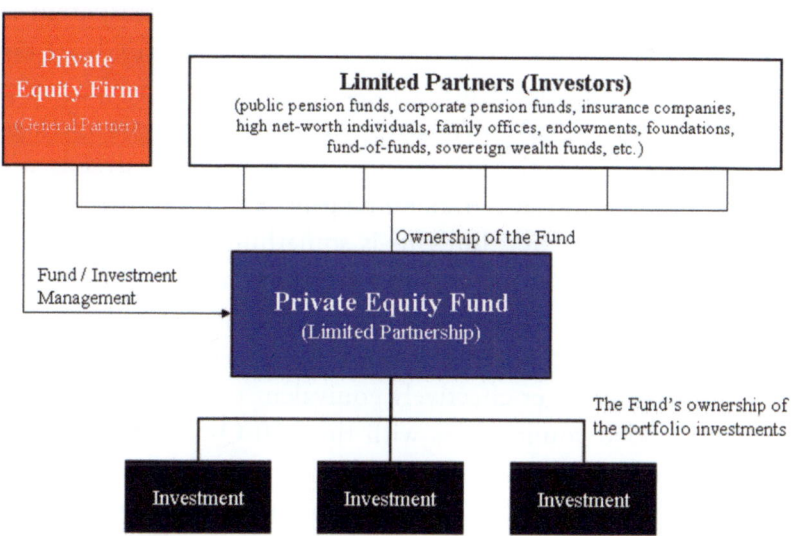

The typical structure of private equity.

SECRET #2: CREATING CAPITAL

In defense of the financial advisor community, and as many will attest, private, or Reg D, funds have a pretty bad reputation in general. Most are poorly managed and don't execute their exit strategy. That being said, as we discussed in the first section, the opportunity to generate substantial risk-adjusted performance can almost only be accomplished in the private fund space (I do know of a rare equities trader or two able to engineer quality risk-adjusted performance with quantitative methods and derivatives strategies). So how do we overcome financial advisors' perceptions about private offerings to give the quality private funds and sponsors that do exist an opportunity to be fairly evaluated by traditional financial distribution channels? Private fund sponsors have to put themselves in the shoes of the due diligence officers and financial advisors who are risking their business by offering their private fund.

Financial advisors are burdened by extraordinary regulatory constraint and potential legal liability that can result in the loss of a highly valuable client, or even their entire practice, if they recommend a bad private investment. This potentially catastrophic outcome is enough to close most financial advisors off to the Reg D space.

Publicly-traded assets are at least ostensibly transparent as mandated by the SEC's registration process. Private funds are not subject to the same rigors and transparency mandates, which makes broker-dealers and RIAs particularly nervous about private offerings. As a matter of fact, the biggest objections financial advisors will typically cite for not recommending private funds to their clients is lack of transparency, but this is something that can be fairly easily rectified if you use a third-party fund administrator, issue quarterly financial reports, and have your fund audited annually by a nationally recognized accounting firm. This gives you as a private fund manager effectively equivalent transparency as your publicly-traded counterparts with their 10-Qs and Ks. Further, communicate in your two-pager and deck how your fund and capital structure are designed to match the liquidity and risk characteristics of the underlying assets and have a due diligence report issued by a reputable third-party firm to inspire confidence in your operational infrastructure and to verify the claims you make in your marketing and offering documents.

Another big objection financial advisors have about private funds is their lack of liquidity. It is true that this is a constraint that regulations make impossible to eliminate completely, but private fund managers should make every effort to minimize the duration of their lock-up period.

One means of accomplishing this is by utilizing an interval fund structure, which is based upon maintaining a fairly large portion of the fund's portfolio in relatively liquid assets to average down the necessary lock-up period as dictated by the most illiquid assets in the portfolio. Of course, great care must be given to this type of fund portfolio construction as the liquid assets could dramatically affect both the risk and return characteristics of the fund.

On the flip side, I'll remind the financial advisors that you're well aware that FINRA expects you to advise any clients with near-term liquidity needs—as in less than a year or so—to be allocated in money markets. If you're advising your clients on capital markets allocations, insofar as the lock-up period of a quality private fund does not conflict with their longer-term liquidity constraints, the allocation decision should be based upon quantitative risk-adjusted performance measures. Of course, private securities that lack liquidity should pay a liquidity premium, but what should that premium be?

It just so happens that Aswath Damodaran, Professor of Finance at the Stern School of Business at NYU, is well versed in private company valuations and illiquidity premiums. He cites the research on the subject to reveal that after all of the noise is cleared, in general, the fair illiquidity premium of a private company relative to its public counterpart is a less than 10%, while the remaining 20–25% discount commonly seen is purely a function of poor management (think mom-and-pop restaurants). For professionally managed private companies and institutional-grade private funds, an 11.1% illiquidity premium on expected returns is very fair.

Another way of illustrating this point is that the S&P 500 has generated an average return of 7.77% percent over the last 14 years as of the printing of this book. If all 500 companies simultaneously went private tomorrow, they would lose approximately 10% of their fundamental value yielding a liquidity-adjusted expected return of 8.63%, a mere 86 basis-point difference.

Private fund sponsors should be clear about the illiquidity premium associated with their fund in addition to its risk-adjusted performance characteristics as measured across a minimum of one complete market cycle and be fully prepared to communicate it.

Hedge Funds

A hedge fund is a common example of a private investment company. Hedge funds are actively managed in an effort to reduce or hedge risk, but the term has come to be used fairly loosely to describe many different types of investment approaches.

Assets/an investment strategy are purchased/executed by a business entity (LLC or LP), the fund, that is managed by a second entity (LLC or LP), the management firm.

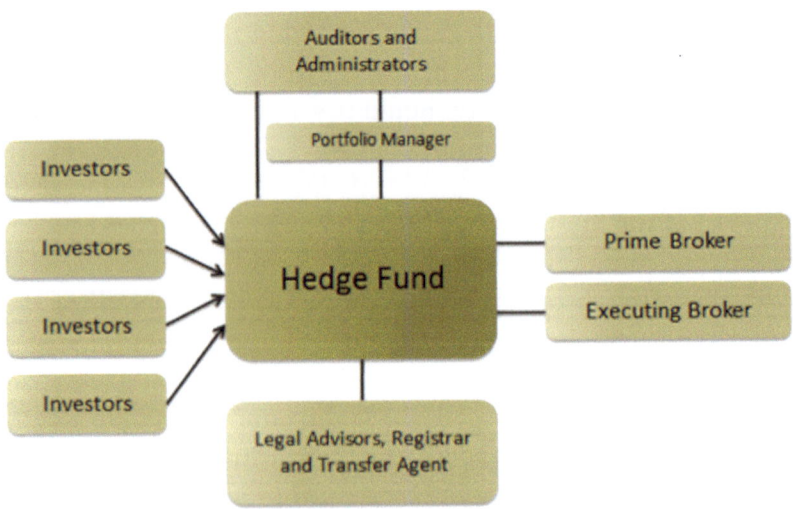

The typical hedge fund structure.

The management firm is generally compensated on what is called a 2&20 structure meaning that the management firm takes 2% of the total assets under management, or AUM, per year paid monthly, known as the management fee, in addition to 20% of the investment gains at the end of each fiscal year, known as the performance fee. Those percentages can vary from firm to firm. The management fee allows the management firm to cover overhead expenses (such as salaries, legal/compliance, accounting/reporting, office space, etc.), while the performance fee incentivizes the management firm to generate superior returns.

Many financial advisors and due diligence firms focus on the fee structure a management firm charges its fund in deciding whether the fund is worthwhile. This is shortsighted. If one fund has generated double-digit returns for the past twenty consecutive years and charges higher fees than another fund that's struggled to keep pace with the market, which one is better? To accurately evaluate a fund, historical performance must be viewed net of fees, regardless of what those fees might be. If the risk-adjusted performance net of fees (again, as measured across a minimum of one complete market cycle) is good, the fund is good, no matter what the fees are.

In terms of private alternative assets, true hedge funds, by definition, are the only asset class that predicates their investment models on quantitative risk metrics. The problem with hedge funds is that few, and I mean very few, generate true portable alpha, and most have fared very poorly in their attempt to bet against the Fed since the 2008 financial crisis. Of the few that have done well, most have only done so of late and simply report quantitative performance over relatively short time periods (i.e., less than one complete market cycle), and expect their investors to take a flier on very fat tailed market risk. As a result, the financial advisors who do have some awareness of quantitative analysis dismiss the risk-adjusted reporting of these hedge funds as largely meaningless, and rightfully so.

Further, when the finance industry thinks about hedge funds, it doesn't tend to think of them in the general sense. Less sophisticated financial firms tend to think of hedge funds as nothing more than a long-short strategy. Other financial firms at least recognize that there's more than one well-established strategy type, but even this perspective misses the point. Here are the nine most-established boxes financial firms will try to pigeonhole all hedge funds into:

1. Long-Short Funds
    a. Market Neutral Funds
    b. Convertible Arbitrage Funds
2. Event-Driven Funds
3. Macro Funds
4. Distressed Securities Funds
5. Emerging Market Funds
6. Long Funds
7. Short Funds
8. Fixed-Income Arbitrage Funds
9. Merger Arbitrage Funds

A hedge fund is not a particular strategy, just like the word "car" does not refer to one particular make and model. As a matter of fact, when Tesla came out, an entirely new form of car entered the market that was different from all the categories of car that existed before it. What would have happened to Tesla if it had to fit into one of those pre-existing categories in order to be sold? If traditional financial product distribution culture had the same influence over the automotive industry that it does over financial products, the Model S would have never been considered a car. "What do you mean it doesn't require gasoline? We don't sell golf carts." This is what traditional financial distribution does to innovative fund managers.

If you engineer a strategy that does a great job of hedging risk, but it doesn't fit into one of these nine boxes, financial distribution firms will have a hard time understanding it and will typically pass. In addition to the fact that we proactively engineer the structure of our financial products to optimize risk-adjusted performance, this is one of the reasons we categorize the funds we create as structured products. The industry still has an expectation that structured products are a fairly specific thing: fixed-income instruments created by layering options over an index, but there is a bit more willingness to accept that the structure might not strictly conform to the familiar.

As I mentioned earlier, hedge funds have established a bit of a bad reputation since 2008 as many have bet against the Fed since then and lost, but I still know of one or two that have done an outstanding job.

Fund of Funds

What if you don't have an investment strategy or asset management business of your own? If you have relationships with high-net-worth individuals and/or the marketing wherewithal to aggregate such, you can establish your business as a capital provider for other quality asset managers as a fund of funds.

For those whose skills and resources are oriented towards marketing, relationship building, sales, and ultimately, capital aggregation, a fund of funds can be a perfect solution. Funds of funds are managed by those who don't have an investment model of their own, but who can aggregate capital and access other well-managed funds that do.

The process of setting up and running a fund of funds is almost identical to the process of establishing a fund to capitalize your own assets management business. The primary difference is that instead of sourcing and managing individual assets, your efforts are focused on sourcing other asset managers who are able to achieve competitive risk-adjusted performance.

SECRET #2: CREATING CAPITAL

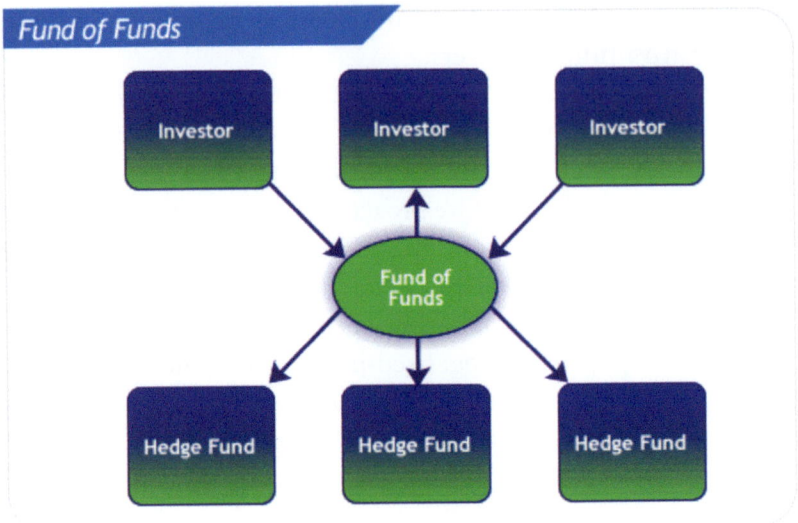

The structure of a fund of funds.

A fund of funds, or feeder fund, can be a great solution for financial advisors as well. A significant challenge associated with 3(c)1 and 3(c)7 funds are the relatively high minimums as dictated by the 100-investor cap and qualified purchaser status mandate, respectively. Given the industry heuristic dictating that only 10% to 15% of a portfolio should be allocated to alternatives and that quality private funds typically have minimums in excess of $1 million, such funds become out of reach for most retail investors. A $1 million minimum for a single private fund would require the investor to have approximately $10 million of investable assets, and this wouldn't allow for any diversification of the alternatives portfolio. This results in the need for individual investors to have around $100 million of investable assets to construct a diversified alternatives portfolio of quality private funds. This problem can be greatly mitigated by a feeder fund structure: the financial advisor establishes a single private fund that holds all his clients' alternatives allocations. That feeder fund, which now holds approximately 10% of all his clients' capital in aggregate, can then use this larger concentrated pool of capital to diversify across a number of quality private alternatives and generate additional, well-deserved fees for the advisor.

For those of you who are not financial advisors but have an established high-net-worth network, wouldn't it be great to be able to compliantly provide them better financial products than what they can find anywhere else and profit handsomely in the process? This is almost certainly a much more lucrative way of both serving and monetizing your relationships than any other service or product you could possibly provide!

DELAWARE STATUTORY TRUSTS

The quickest and least expensive way for real estate asset managers who have saturated their friends and family network to scale their business quickly is by securitizing their portfolio of stabilized assets under a series of Delaware Statutory Trusts, or DSTs.

DSTs are trusts established under the laws of the state of Delaware and may confer an undivided interest in a common piece of real property to more than 35 investors, which qualifies under Section 1031 of the Internal Revenue Code as a tax-deferred exchange. DST ownership essentially offers the same benefits and risks that an investor would receive as a single large-scale investment property owner, but without the management responsibility.

In 2004, the IRS blessed DSTs with an official Revenue Ruling affording the specific structure like-kind status for the purpose of replacement property under a 1031 exchange. The Revenue Ruling (Rev. Ruling 2004-86) permits the DST to own 100% of the fee-simple interest in the underlying real estate and may allow up to 100 investors, sometimes more, to participate as beneficial owners of the property.

- DSTs are a product of necessity driven by investors' need to roll over 1031 proceeds and are best suited for distribution through the independent broker-dealer space.

SECRET #2: CREATING CAPITAL

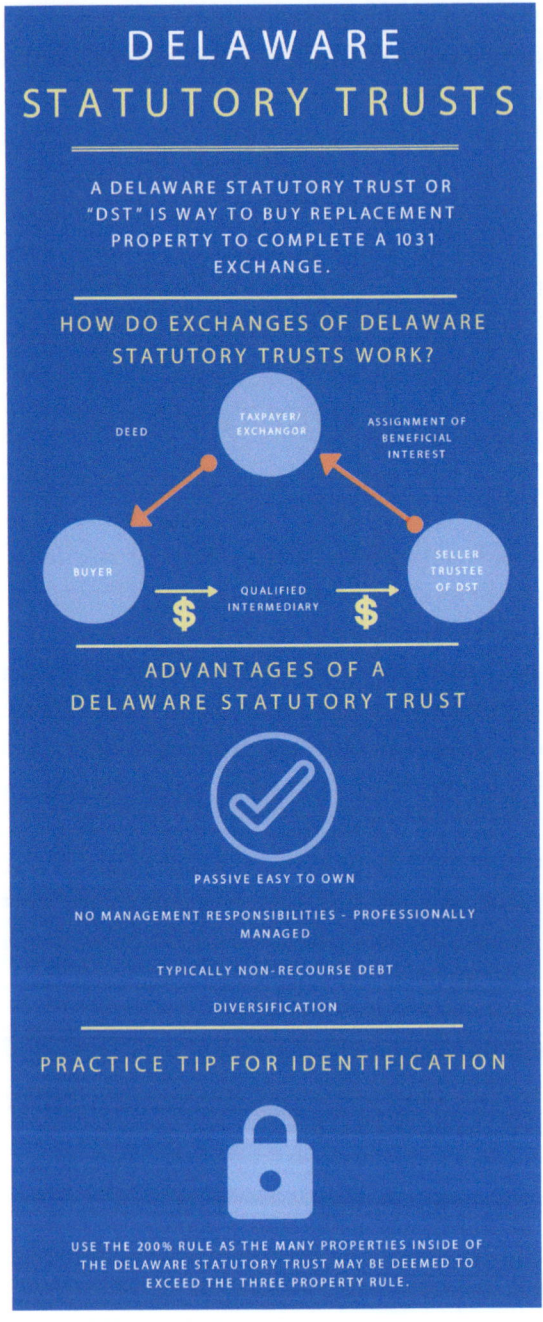

The Delaware Statutory Trust.

- In 2018, over $2B was raised across 35 sponsors with an approximate $20 million average equity offering per DST.

- A sponsor's first DST will typically require 6 months to complete the capital raise (after all documents are drafted and administration established); the second: 3–5 months, and each DST thereafter typically requires 2–4 months to fully fund.

Because DSTs are a product of necessity and carry relatively low idiosyncratic risk, the broker-dealer community is keen to host them on their platform, which makes them a great vehicle for real estate asset managers to quickly scale their business.

CREATING & SELLING PRIVATE SECURITIES BASICS

Let's start diving into the specifics of private fund creation and securities issuance. Once you establish your investment model and determine your capital structure, you'll need to have the offering and marketing documents drafted to communicate the details in both legal and user-friendly terms.

Offering Documents (To Create and Sell Shares in the Fund)

- Private placement memorandum/offering memorandum, or PPM/OM – Discloses risk considerations and describes management firm, compensation, investment approach, and offering terms

- Operating agreement (for fund) – Details the structure and terms of fund

- Subscription agreement – Is the contract for the purchase and sales of shares in the fund

Marketing Documents

- Summary/two-pager/sell sheet/fact card
- Presentation/slide deck/pitch book

Legal Compliance Considerations (1933 Act)

- While there are legal exceptions, such as crowdfunding, 506(c), and Reg A+ offerings, private securities should not be advertised to the general public, and investors should be accredited as defined by the SEC to mean they have a net worth of at least $1 million (not including primary residence) and/or make at least $200k per year and/or $300k per year as a married couple.

- The management firm must file Form D - Notice of Exempt Offering of Securities with the SEC (in addition to Form PF if you are already an SEC-registered RIA) upon selling any shares in its fund. If the fund invests in securities, the management firm may be required to register as an investment adviser.

As I mentioned earlier, the '33 Act and Reg D are not the only legal constraints on private funds. Funds exempt from registration under 3(c)1 of the 40 Act are capped at 100 investors including the manager; the 3(c)5c exemption allows for real estate funds only; and under 3(c)7, all investors must be qualified purchasers, which means, in general, that they must have $5 million of investable assets as an individual or $25 million as an entity.

In addition to the offering and marketing documents I just went over, if you're pursuing distribution through broker-dealers and RIAs, you'll also likely need a third-party due-diligence report, an internally produced due diligence questionnaire, or DDQ, and a Committee on Uniform Security Identification Procedures, or CUSIP, number.

So far, we've established that you first have to be able to generate, measure, and report quality risk-adjusted performance and then second, package that performance under a well-designed capital structure to create a quality investment product. The third piece of the puzzle is to establish the operational rigor required to be considered a responsible steward of other people's money by the gatekeepers of the capital markets.

At least one, but usually all three of these considerations are lacking in the potential clients we come across, regardless of the amount of experience they have. Let's take a look at two common client profiles we encounter: 1) the seasoned syndicator, and 2) the newbie. Each group always has the same objections out of the gate. The newbies don't think they're ready for this level of sophistication, and the seasoned syndicators are like, "I've been doing this a long time; I don't need help." The truth of the matter is that you all do.

RAISING MONEY – THE TALE OF TWO TYPICAL CLIENT PROFILES

Here are the typical issues we see for each group:

The Seasoned Syndicator

- Limited by the appetite retail/passive investors have for real estate
- Relies on personal relationships
- May utilize crowdfunding
- Typically, overpays for money
- Usually unwittingly breaks the law in raising money
- Typically, unwittingly overleveraged and hampered by debt service

One of our first clients had been in business for over 15 years and raised over $100 million. It wasn't until year 13 that they were informed of their illegal issuance of debt securities by a few individual states and the SEC, which compounded their existing problem of being insolvent. They didn't realize they were carrying too much expensive debt until a couple deals out of the hundreds they had done didn't go as planned (and this was during a strong market). The moral of this story is that real estate experience does not equal competence within the complex game of managing other people's money.

The Newbie

- Often has never even considered managing a fund before
- Tends to think only in terms of debt and is subject to lenders
- Typically overpays for money
- Often struggles to capture quality deal flow (loses to the established veterans) without readily accessible capital

It is far less expensive to start out doing things the right way than it is to make costly and potentially career-ending mistakes by doing things poorly. The best-case scenario is that you survive the early stages of growth only to have to completely restructure your entire business when you decide you want to gain serious scale, if you even make it that far.

The Newbies

Those just starting out in the asset management business—and that includes anyone from active real estate investors to hedge fund managers—can find it nigh impossible to overcome all of the hurdles that stand between developing an initial investment model and scaling it into a legitimate financial institution with hundreds of millions of dollars in assets under management; but Adagio's business is to ensure our client asset managers do just that.

Imagine what it will be like when you no longer have to submit to anyone else for money, when you not only control vast amounts of capital, but have earned a genuine sense of pride in knowing that you have become a one-in-a-million expert on money and business that can go toe-to-toe with the very top of the financial services industry. Isn't that something worth pursuing?

Here's what the first steps of that path look like:

- We position our clients to raise equity capital without giving up control and low-cost debt on their terms.

- To accomplish that, we work with them to rigorously construct a theoretical track record that allows for meaningful back-tested performance. In other words, even if they don't have a portfolio directly managed under a specific investment model, we ethically and compliantly allow them to show what it would have looked like if they had.

- The lessons they learn along the way enable them to out-compete well-established market participants with capital on demand, better structure, and portfolio construction skills.

- While it may sound complex, the learning curve isn't much steeper than what it takes to learn how to evaluate good real estate deals or various equities trading strategies. We take the securities issuance and regulatory requirements off their plate, which is far and away the most difficult part of the process.

The Seasoned Syndicators

For the veterans who have been raising money for some time and are seen as the authority within their domain: as you're probably aware, there are much higher levels to achieve. The goal, as far

SECRET #2: CREATING CAPITAL

as we're concerned, is not to be the lord of your fiefdom; it's to compete with the likes of Blackstone.

Raising money for individual projects is one thing; it's something entirely different to manage a portfolio that is not dependent upon institutional debt and can be securitized to compete with the best financial products in the market. Our clients have consistently raised between $5 and $50 million per month by selling financial performance that retail investors were unable to acquire through traditional channels, and they still have a tremendous amount of room for improvement.

This is what the process of being our client looks like:

- We optimize their risk-adjusted performance through revising their investment model, operations, and capital structure utilizing derivatives as appropriate.

- We then create the distribution channels that provide our clients with both direct and indirect access to the capital markets, which represents about $20 trillion starved for low-risk fixed-income yield and quality risk-adjusted growth. It's like selling water in the desert.

- We restructure their asset management business as an institutional-grade fund or structured product to meet the different types of retail investor demand. Some people, like retirees, need fixed-income and others need growth. We work with our clients to create better versions of both.

- In short, we graduate our clients from raising money to distributing strategically designed financial assets through us.

Isn't that level of institutional respect and scale something you've aspired to? It's our job to make it your reality, and that's what we do.

SECRET #2 SUMMARY

This is Joe Maiullo, a Vice President of Middle Markets at Morgan Stanley in New York. When asked about Adagio's method of financial product development and distribution, he described it as an...

"*Innovative solution to form debt and equity capital.*"

JOSEPH MAIULLO, Vice President/Portfolio Manager, Morgan Stanley

...for private alternative asset managers who previously had no legitimate way to access the capital markets.

Morgan Stanley is one of the biggest and most highly regarded investment banks in the world, and I think this comment encapsulates everything that needs to be said about Secret #2, which can be summarized as:

"The quickest way to grow assets is by creating them."
BENJAMIN D. SUMMERS

You're probably thinking that's great, but it sounds way too complicated, right? Well, if you had to go out and hunt for the hidden information you need and figure out how to do all this on your own, it would be. But you don't. I've shown you exactly what you need, but if you feel you still need more guidance, we still have one more section to cover: Secret #3.

Secret #3
Navigating Regulatory Compliance

The shadow banking secret to keeping you compliant and protect you from liability as you scale your investment business...

INTRODUCTION TO SECURITIES LAW

While the original motivation of securities laws and regulations may have been to protect the public, today they primarily serve a much different function. Securities laws are written by lobbyists for the big banks with the intent of stifling competition. The more regulation that exists, the more cost-prohibitive it is for small competitors to enter the market. Startup compliance and legal expenses alone run hundreds of thousands of dollars for securities issuers.

Because many alternative asset managers such as real estate operators are not licensed by FINRA, they don't know what they don't know with respect to securities law and compliance. As a result, most real estate investors who use "other people's money" are inadvertently breaking the law, regardless of how many decades of experience they may have.

THE WOODBRIDGE CASE STUDY

Here's one example that really captures the hidden but dramatic time bomb created by confidence in ignorance developed through the illusion of "long-term" success.

Woodbridge was one of the biggest private real estate investors in the country that had grown to manage over $1 billion in assets. The problem was that they unwittingly built their entire business on illegal securities issuance and a probably well-intentioned, but irresponsible capital structure that ultimately turned into a Ponzi scheme and bankrupted them at the peak of the market.

We reached out to Woodbridge several times to help right their ship in the years before all this went down, but they didn't think they needed us at the time we could have been effective. We were provided legal opinions by reputable law firms that defended their securities issuance practices. By the time they were willing to listen, it was too late; the SEC had already cornered them. One of the many takeaways here is that while there are a fair number of law firms claiming to do private securities work, only very few are truly competent in that arena.

Unfortunately, this is not an isolated incident. There are several other similar firms we're aware of that have either already arrived at or are en route to the exact same outcome along an almost identical path. And just like Woodbridge, a combination of confidence in ignorance and too much inertia in the wrong direction prevent them from heeding good advice.

I'm tired of hearing, "I've been successfully doing this for a long time; I'm safe." No, you're not. Whether or not you're following the law dictates whether you're safe. The fact that you've been unwittingly getting away with breaking the law for a long time is simply no evidence of a well-run business.

Now, you can only imagine what kind of laws are being broken and financial best practices are being violated by the small startups trying to raise money. It's tough, I get it, but you have to do things the right way. Otherwise, sooner or later, things will end badly.

THE WOODBRIDGE CASE STUDY

Real Estate Developer Woodbridge Group Files for Bankruptcy Amid SEC's Fraud Probe

By **Dawn McCarty**
December 4, 2017, 7:12 AM EST *Updated on* December 4, 2017, 11:19 AM EST

→ SEC said in October it was looking at CEO's ties to affiliates
→ Firm sells commercial mortgage stakes and Aspen properties

Woodbridge Group of Companies LLC, a high-end real estate developer, filed for bankruptcy amid the departure of its chief executive and an investigation into potential securities fraud linked to $1 billion in investments.

The Chapter 11 filing on Monday in U.S. Bankruptcy Court in Wilmington, Delaware, cited "unforeseen costs associated with ongoing litigation and regulatory compliance." The U.S. Securities and Exchange Commission has been probing whether Woodbridge defrauded investors who invested more than $1 billion. The agency also sought more information on about 236 limited liability companies Woodbridge formed, according to an October SEC court filing.

THE WALL STREET JOURNAL

BANKRUPTCY

Real Estate Developer Woodbridge Group Files for Bankruptcy
Company is being questioned by the SEC on its fundraising practices

By *Peg Brickley*
Updated Dec. 4, 2017 2:08 p.m. ET

Real-estate developer Woodbridge Group of Companies has filed for chapter 11 bankruptcy protection as it grapples with questions about its fundraising practices from the Securities and Exchange Commission.

Bloomberg and *The Wall Street Journal* reporting
on the bankruptcy of Woodbridge Group.

To become financially independent, you have no choice but to raise capital from others; there really is no other way. You just better make sure you know what you're doing and have the

SECRET #3: NAVIGATING REGULATORY COMPLIANCE

right counsel in place because the consequences are too dire if you don't. Don't let what you don't know cause you the same avoidable fate experienced by the likes of Woodbridge.

A FEW SECURITIES LAW CONSIDERATIONS COMMONLY IGNORED BY UNLICENSED ISSUERS

We've established that securities laws are extremely complex and even vague. Here's a brief list of some commonly ignored securities law considerations that expose a lot of unwitting issuers to tremendous legal risk:

- Debt instruments (i.e., including mortgage loans) used for the purpose of generating investment income are securities. In other words, if you're borrowing money for your investment business from an entity not FDIC-insured, you're likely issuing securities and subject to securities laws.

- You are not allowed to promise any particular return (as in implying no risk) in your marketing; that is considered fraud.

- When you issue private securities, you are required to file Form D with the SEC.

- Real estate can be defined as a security, and if you manage a real estate fund, you may be required to register with the SEC as an investment adviser.

- Syndicators issuing securities under the Reg D 506(c) exemption ("crowdfunding") must verify the accredited status of every purchaser, and non-real estate funds with an incentive allocation (aka "promote" or "performance fee") can only accept up to 100 qualified clients, or all must be qualified purchasers.

- If you've ever been cited for behavior as listed under Rule 506(d) that defines a "bad actor," you are prohibited from issuing private securities.

- If you knowingly break securities laws, you can go to jail.

- Most attorneys have different interpretations of securities laws.

If you ask five different attorneys to interpret a complex securities issue, you'll get five different opinions. Ask me how I know...

BROKER-DEALER, RIA & FAMILY OFFICE ESOTERIC CONSIDERATIONS

Here are a few considerations that can help broker-dealers, RIAs, and family offices mitigate their regulatory and liability risk while better serving their clients.

1. Measuring the risk-adjusted performance of alternative assets across a minimum of one complete market cycle can be the most effective way to not only serve your clients but to keep lawsuits and the regulators at bay.

2. Feeder funds/entities can be utilized to compliantly provide clients diversified access to quality alternatives that have otherwise prohibitive minimum investment thresholds.

3. FINRA has stated that there is an inherent conflict of interest in having sponsors pay for third-party due diligence reports, which exposes most broker-dealers to potential regulatory risk. Consider joining or forming a consortium to share the costs associated with third-party due diligence reports required on alternative sponsors that include quantitative risk measures across a minimum of one complete market cycle.

THE INVESTMENT CLUB—AN UNDERUTILIZED FEEDER STRUCTURE

As I previously alluded to, regardless of the merit of the offering, it can be surprisingly difficult to sell quality private securities through traditional financial distribution channels: broker-dealers and Registered Investment Advisers, or RIAs. Why is it so difficult? Broker-dealers are typically motivated by regulatory fear (that is only exacerbated by most alternatives) and their transaction-based fees often break the economics of alternative offerings. Retail advisors are indoctrinated to dismiss private securities due to their perceived lack of transparency and liquidity. They're also inundated with wholesalers pushing shoddy product on them.

That being said, it's worth noting that there's been an interesting trend over the past couple decades. The number of publicly-traded companies has been cut in half as regulatory pressure and market drivers have pushed more and more of the capital markets into private equity. To be fair, the regulators are squeezing all sides of the market, not just private issuers.

The good news is that there's a compliant, alternative means for private securities issuers to bypass traditional financial distribution channels to access retail investors: responsibly administered investment clubs. They can benefit securities issuers, unlicensed relationship builders who want to both help and monetize their network, and retail investors alike.

Before I dive into all of the benefits, there are a few misconceptions about investment clubs that I should get out of the way:

1. Investment clubs cannot advertise for new membership

2. Investment clubs cannot hold over $25 million in assets

3. Investment clubs cannot have over 100 members

These false beliefs generally come from a casual reading of the SEC's publication Investment Clubs and the SEC (https://

THE INVESTMENT CLUB—AN UNDERUTILIZED FEEDER STRUCTURE

www.sec.gov/reportspubs/investor-publications/investorpubsinvclubhtm.html) and may only be true if the investment club's membership interests are structured as securities, which effectively turns the club into a fund and makes it subject to the '40 Act. We make sure the clubs we work with are clearly not operating as private funds, which removes these constraints.

Investment clubs (as recognized by the SEC) can be organized by anyone (no licensing required) and facilitate access to top-performing private securities for both accredited and non-accredited investors. You can profit by utilizing them to compliantly aggregate other retail investors to invest in quality private funds and afford yourself access to these funds in the process.

Here's the legal basis for investment clubs:

- Under the Investment Advisers Act of 1940, §202(a)(11), teachers are specifically excluded from the definition of Investment Adviser. This exclusion allows for general financial advice to be provided by unlicensed individuals insofar as it is incidental to an educational program. Educational programs can be utilized to both market club membership and provide ongoing value to members in support of their shared interest to recognize appropriate, quality financial products, which ultimately guides the club's investment decisions.

- Under the Securities Act of 1933, CFR §230 Reg. D Rule 501(a)(3), any business with total assets in excess of $5 million not formed for the purpose of acquiring a specific security is defined to be an accredited investor. In other words, the investment clubs themselves become accredited investors when they aggregate $5 million; and when they hit $25 million of investable assets, they become qualified purchasers. As long as no more than 40% of the club's assets are allocated to one particular fund, it is clear of being deemed as formed for the purpose of investing in any one fund. Why is the 40%

threshold important? If the club were deemed to be formed for the purpose of investing in any given fund, the regulators would look through the club to evaluate the status of its individual members and potentially force the fund to register with the SEC, which could be catastrophic for the fund.

- The SEC, in its publication Investment Clubs and the SEC (January 13, 2016), has specifically verified that membership in investment clubs is not a security interest insofar as all members are active (by vote) in the decisions of the club.

One of the biggest advantages of utilizing the investment club structure deals with advertising. Because club membership, when properly structured and administered, is not considered a security, there is no federal prohibition on general solicitation or advertising for membership. That allows for innovative marketing strategies to communicate the unique benefits of membership and aggregate AUM—strategies that we've studied extensively, continue to utilize and have proven highly effective.

That being said, it is important to note there are some state-level regulations that you must make yourself aware of to compliantly form an investment club in your area.

Investment clubs afford financial advisors, independent insurance agents, IRA custodians, accountants, real estate brokers, and marketing professionals the opportunity to compliantly provide their clients—accredited, qualified, or otherwise—exclusive access to superior investment products and profit in the process. The ability to offer this service gives you a competitive advantage that can be compliantly integrated into your overall marketing and client recruitment efforts.

Can you see the advantages of being able to pool unlimited money into accredited and qualified entities without being subject to the legal burden of managing a fund or securities brokerage?

SECRET #3 SUMMARY

"When it comes to compliance, what you don't know can hurt you—and badly. While maintaining competent compliance counsel is critical, the most powerful compliance (and growth) tool at your disposal is the motivation to do the right thing simply because it's the right thing to do. As a byproduct of applying this maxim, continuous improvement and growth will inevitably follow."

BENJAMIN D. SUMMERS

The third shadow banking secret to keep you compliant and protect you from liability as you scale your investment business is first to acknowledge that you don't know what you don't know, and second, to make sure that you're working with competent professionals to ensure you're in compliance and maximizing your growth opportunities.

As a bonus, investment clubs can serve as a perfect solution for licensed and unlicensed professionals alike to compliantly aggregate capital from both accredited and non-accredited investors without subjecting themselves to the burden of securities regulations.

Imagine how many people you know, or clients you have, or targets of your marketing campaigns who would love to be able to access substantially better investments than what are peddled through your run-of-the-mill financial advisors and online brokerages—and not be forced into volatile crypto and poorly managed real estate as the only alternative. Wouldn't you like to be the only professional in their sphere who can compliantly provide them what they desperately need simply by setting up an investment club?

And for you financial advisors who want to do better, how much would it help you differentiate your firm if you were able to confidently vet sponsors and provide your clients access to exclusive products that are demonstrably better by every established objective measure than what's recommended and sold by your competition?

Let's start bringing it all together.

Applying the Three Secrets & Tailored Solutions

BUY SIDE VS. SELL SIDE—A ROLE FOR EVERYONE

Sell side financial firms, such as broker-dealers, essentially sell ideas to their clients, and in most cases, these ideas are communicated for free.

Buy side financial firms essentially have a pool of capital to use for investing, as is the case with RIAs and hedge funds.

We can say that sell side entities provide services to buy side entities. The goal of the sell side is to close the deal, whereas, the goal of the buy side is to generate risk-adjusted returns that beat the market (i.e., *alpha*) for their clients.

While it is illegal to act as a broker without a license, there is no prohibition on selling assets you own, whether they are physical properties or securities you issue (albeit with some exceptions). Further, interests in investment clubs are not deemed to be securities by the SEC, which means involvement in one does not require FINRA licensing.

Everyone participates in the finance industry, from dumb money 401k owners and entrepreneurs to smart money shadow banks. What role are you going to play?

How does it feel to know that you can access as much money as you can responsibly put to work in your investment business and that your portfolio is protected from the next financial crisis?

As an investment adviser, how does it feel to be able to afford your clients access to exclusive financial products that meet their income and growth needs with the confidence they won't lose when the markets take a hit? How would it help you grow your business if you were able to objectively measure and clearly communicate the merits of your advice?

Both of those aspirations are attainable, but the only way to achieve either of them is to actually apply the three secrets we've just discussed.

1. Measure risk-adjusted performance to manage your investment portfolio to better performance than what is otherwise available.

2. Create a fund that allows others to participate in your investment portfolio's performance in ways that meet their individual investment goals.

3. Legally issue shares (or debt) in your fund without fear of the regulators to profit from hundreds of millions of dollars in your portfolio.

U.S. Bureau of Engraving and Printing: $100 Federal Reserve Notes.

If you're not a financial advisor and don't have a quality asset management business of your own, form an investment club to compliantly aggregate the capital of your clients, followers and relationships providing them access to better investments than what they can find anywhere else.

Have a look at the ABL annual returns vs. the industry benchmarks. Who wouldn't want to achieve that level of performance?

Annual Returns

	ABL	S&P 500	MSCI US REIT
2007	26.32%	5.49%	-16.82%
2008	32.07%	-37.00%	-37.97%
2009	41.56%	26.46%	28.61%
2010	26.32%	15.06%	28.48%
2011	27.71%	2.11%	8.69%
2012	33.36%	16.00%	17.77%
2013	25.96%	32.39%	2.47%
2014	20.93%	13.69%	30.38%
2015	27.26%	1.38%	25.20%
Average *	**28.94%**	**6.40%**	**6.92%**

Adagio ABL, S&P 500, and MSCI US REIT Indices annual returns from 2007 to 2015.

You're not going to achieve these results by following the herd of financial advisors or listening to other syndicators, and you're not going to "friends and family" your way to your growth goals.

On the flip side, financial advisors can't protect their clients' downside exposure through random diversification, mutual funds, or by ignoring alternative assets.

There are over $20 trillion starved for genuinely low-risk real yield in fixed income and an escape from the ever-looming drop in stocks and questionable real estate funds, but no one is differentiating themselves with any substantive solutions. Now, you can.

What if you could capture 1% of that? $200 billion is there for the taking. Would that be worth improving the way you do business? What about only 10 basis points worth? Would $20 billion be worth it? What about only 1 basis point? Is $2 billion worth it? What about 1/100th of a basis point (0.0001%)? That's still $20 million. Worth it? The money is out there and desperate for objectively measured low-risk yield.

How would that kind of growth change your self-image… earning the sense of pride in knowing that you're doing things better, and serving your investors in the way they came to you to be helped.

I've just given you everything you need. Can't you see how applying what we've just covered will allow you to achieve your professional, personal, and financial goals?

I've given you the opportunity of a lifetime to bring merit to the finance industry—whether you're already a financial professional or not. Why not take advantage of it and get paid handsomely for your effort?

Are you feeling a little overwhelmed by all of this new information? Depending upon your current level of expertise, you probably want additional help to master and implement the skills and information we've just covered. I sincerely want to make the investment industry better for everyone involved because there's so much opportunity for improvement and growth.

I know many of you come from very different backgrounds and have experience with different facets of various industries that participate in the financial markets. To affect the greatest positive impact on the industry, I've developed a series of tailored solutions to meet each of your individual needs and goals.

Everything we do has evolved from the perspective of the needs of the retail investor and every merit-seeking investor. While the process may be complex, analogous to the iPhone, the end result is a user-friendly experience for all that cuts out the noise to address the needs associated with all three fundamental variables of investing: risk, return, and liquidity.

Here's a list of the various market participants and the tailored solutions we've developed for each based upon their feedback to us over the years. I'll briefly go over each of them.

FINANCIAL ADVISORS

(family offices, RIAs, broker-dealers, and due diligence officers)

Third-Party Risk Analytics Services

- Quantify the risk of your portfolio

- Vet sponsors and asset managers
- Identify risk-adjusted performance in new markets

Private Structured Products

- Provide your clients with investments that generate superior risk-adjusted performance
- Open-end, institutional-grade, risk-engineered, private fixed income, and equity structures
- Alternative underlying assets
- 1 to 60-month lock-up periods
- Positive alpha and low loss potential (as measured since January 2007 or earlier)
- Quarterly reporting, annual audits, and third-party administration

Feeder Fund and Investment Club Services

- Provide all of your clients access to diversified, quality, transparent alternative assets

For financial advisors, our services are designed to address the two biggest problems you face: regulatory/legal liability and the need to economically grow your client base.

The variables considered by financial advisors and capital markets investors in their attempt to account for risk—such as asset class, diversification, offering cost structure, cap rate, geographical market, leverage ratio, etc.—all contribute to the probability of an asset or portfolio losing value, but none of these tell you the actual probability of loss.

That's where Adagio comes in. We are able to measure the risk-adjusted performance of everything you touch: from each individual asset, public or private, to the portfolios you construct for your clients. We quantify the risk of your portfolios, vet sponsors and asset managers, and identify risk-adjusted performance in new markets. Not only does this help you identify which assets are most likely to harm your clients, but it also allows you to clearly communicate your competitive advantage in objective terms. That is our Third-Party Risk Analytics Services.

As discussed earlier, Adagio Institute is a public charity dedicated to financial education, and Adagio Capital Management is an investment adviser and fund manager. At this time, we do not provide financial advice to the retail market, but the institute's educational initiatives attract many retail investors looking for advisors who share our risk management perspective. As a part of our public service mandate, we have an obligation to send them somewhere. So, we do—to financial advisors who demonstrate the ability to measure and manage risk with the same rigor we do. The advisors that we are able to identify with certainty that are doing such are the ones who utilize our risk analytics services, so they are the beneficiaries of these referrals. They are plentiful, and many are high-net-worth.

Also, we create tailored and transparent private structured products that meet the risk-adjusted performance demands of your clients that can't otherwise be met.

- They are open-end, institution-grade, risk-engineered, private fixed income and equity structures.
- They are constructed on alternative underlying assets.
- Their lock-up periods generally range from 1 to 60-months to meet a variety of liquidity demands.
- They generate positive alpha and low loss potential, as measured since January 2007 or earlier.
- They report quarterly, are audited annually, and utilize third-party administration.

I want to emphasize that we are not in the business of selling funds. We're in the business of serving financial advisors and other intermediaries by providing third-party risk analytics services to assist them in gaining a meaningful understanding of the risk profile of the assets on their platforms and creating financial products that fill holes in their platforms with respect to performance and liquidity. This effort requires two-way communication. You tell us what you have and what your clients need; we measure what you have and do our best to construct products to meet those needs.

If all of your clients are accredited, we can work with you to develop a feeder entity that allows for greater diversification of their alternatives portfolio. If you have unaccredited and non-qualified clients, we can work with you to facilitate the establishment of investment clubs that compliantly afford them access to quality private offerings they'd otherwise not be able to see. In other words, we're able to help you provide all of your clients access to superior risk-adjusted performance via quality alternative assets constructed to institutional-grade standards with the highest levels of transparency.

Schedule a complimentary strategy session to discover the appropriate solution for you at www.adagioinstitute.org/schedule.

OTHER FINANCIAL PROFESSIONALS

(independent insurance agents, real estate brokers, IRA custodians, fund administrators, accountants, attorneys, marketers, and relationship builders)

Investment Club Services

- Compliantly provide your clients access to exclusive investment products

- Further monetize your client base with a differentiating and high-demand service

- Provide non-qualified clients and unaccredited investors access to quality alternative assets
- Utilize Adagio's risk-analytics services to measure the quality of the club's assets

To those of you who are non-FINRA-licensed professionals, how many of you have clients looking for an alternative to their financial advisor or poorly managed real estate syndications but feel limited in how you are legally allowed to help them? I know some of you were burned by the likes of Woodbridge and are fearful of the repercussion of the harm done to your clients, fearful of potential legal action, fearful of the loss of revenue, and fearful of how to evaluate similar offerings. We can help you assuage all of those fears with the investment club structure.

Schedule a complimentary strategy session to discover the appropriate solution for you at www.adagioinstitute.org/schedule.

RETAIL AND INSTITUTIONAL INVESTORS

(qualified purchasers, qualified clients, accredited investors, and non-accredited savers)

As mentioned earlier, it is the perspective of the retail investor that has motivated everything we've done since we got started in 2005 to address the shortcomings of the financial services industry and provide investors merit-based, substantive products and services. I'm very proud of what we've been able to accomplish in that regard. By extension, any investor, including large institutional allocators, seeking quality assets and objective, meaningful, risk-adjusted performance can benefit from our work. Here's an overview of what we can do for you:

Third-Party Risk Analytics
- Evaluate the risk-adjusted performance of any financial advisor, portfolio, or asset you are considering

Investment Club Membership (For Non-Accredited/ Non-Qualified Retail Investors/Individuals)

- Gain the exclusive access of the top 1% to the best-performing alternative investments
- Get exclusive, invaluable investment educational materials

Private Structured Products (For High-Net-Worth Individuals and Institutions)

- Boost your investment portfolio with measured, superior, risk-adjusted performance
- Open-end, institutional-grade, risk-engineered, private fixed income, and equity structures
- Alternative underlying assets
- 1 to 60-month lock-up period
- Positive alpha and low loss potential (as measured since January 2007 or earlier)
- Quarterly reporting, annual audits, third-party administration

Schedule a complimentary strategy session to discover the appropriate solution for you at www.adagioinstitute.org/schedule.

ALTERNATIVE ASSET MANAGERS/SPONSORS

(hedge fund managers, real estate investors, lenders, and syndicators)

Third-Party Risk Analytics

- Boost your capital raising efforts with measured risk-adjusted performance recognized by broker-dealers, RIAs, and investment clubs

Investment Banking Services for Alternative Asset Managers

- Maximize the potential risk-adjusted performance of your investment strategy
- Fully access the capital markets to raise all of the capital you need
- Ensure your investment business is in full compliance

To serve the investment needs of the public and institutional allocators, we help deserving alternative asset managers maximize their performance and reach their AUM potential.

We provide our risk-analytics services to seasoned asset managers allowing them to communicate the merits of their portfolio in meaningful, objective terms, and we're also able to construct theoretical track records for newer asset managers who have the skill but lack the experience. To construct the theoretical track record, we translate your investment model into a comprehensive set of rules and identify every possible variable associated with those rules that contribute to your overall performance. From there, we plug actual historical data going back to at least January 2007 into each of those variables and weight them accordingly to determine your theoretical historical returns. From there, those returns can be analyzed to determine your risk-adjusted performance characteristics for marketing and distribution purposes.

As a simple anecdotal example that highlights the rigor of our process, in the case of real estate developers, we dive all of the way down into the statistical relationships between their contractors' build estimates and actual times and costs to construct to measure construction risk. The effort we make is comprehensive, and the result is that we provide all asset managers the ability to report their performance, regardless of their tenure, in truly meaningful, comparable terms.

On the investment banking front, qualified asset managers and real estate investors are able to hire us to implement our expertise on their behalf, do all of the work for them to form and distribute a dedicated fund or structured product that fully capitalizes their business, and incur the licensing and regulatory burdens they'd otherwise be responsible for. We consult with them to refine their investment model, capital structure, and operations to become responsible stewards of the public's money and achieve marketable performance. We construct their theoretical track record as needed and backtest it. We securitize their business through the creation of dedicated funds and structured products and build the distribution required to sell those funds and products through the appropriate channels to meet their capital needs. As you might imagine, it's a relatively expensive endeavor—generally upper-six to seven figures—and it can run much higher depending upon the complexity required to get through that process and reach the target AUM. This is the only service of its kind and well worth the effort to raise hundreds of millions of dollars. And even better, as I mentioned earlier, all upfront expenses incurred by our client asset managers are reimbursed by the structures we create to capitalize them at a rate that can be economically supported by those structures. The result is that the entire process becomes ultimately free as our clients only have to float the costs for a finite period.

Schedule a complimentary strategy session to discover the appropriate solution for you at www.adagioinstitute.org/schedule.

THE SHADOW BANKER'S SECRETS PROGRAM

All that being said, I know many people—especially those just starting out—aren't ready to engage us yet, but I genuinely want to see as many market participants as possible doing the right things to dramatically improve their investment portfolios, establish true financial independence, and in the process, change the industry for the better. So, I took a great deal of time to put together a package that would allow those who can't afford our services yet everything they need to be successful. I know it takes size to have significant influence, and I know what's needed for you to achieve size on the scale of 9-figures and beyond. I've seen it, and I've done it.

The Shadow Banker's Secrets Program includes everything you need to successfully create your own shadow bank.

We've done our very best to assemble everything you'll need to implement what we've discussed as a do-it-yourselfer: from educational programs, template documents, and a user-friendly risk-adjusted performance calculator to one-on-one support from me. We call it the Shadow Banker's Secrets Program, and it's incredible.

The first thing I put together was a masterclass: Ben Summers Teaches Investment Banking in Real Estate—How to Compliantly Raise Low-Cost Capital Without Having to Ask for It. While the short title references investment banking in real estate, it's applicable to any asset class or securitized portfolio.

It's a two-and-a-half-hour video recording of a live class with downloadable slides that gives you a high-level overview of "the what" that's required for raising unlimited, low-cost capital as an institutional-grade fund manager. It covers a lot of what is included in this book but with more of a real estate bent. It's meant to serve as an introduction.

Ben Summers teaches investment banking in real estate.

In addition to the masterclass, I developed the AIP course on the Blackboard platform, the same platform used by most major universities for their online courses. While the masterclass gives you "the what," the AIP course gives you "the how." It contains a lot of information, and you can approach it in a couple different ways:

1) You can either treat the course as a reference, looking up what you need as you need it, or

2) You can go through the whole thing in sequence and come out the other side as an Accredited Investment Professional designee. Financial advisors who achieve the Accredited Investment Professional designation—like our risk analytics clients—are eligible to be referred clients by the Adagio Institute.

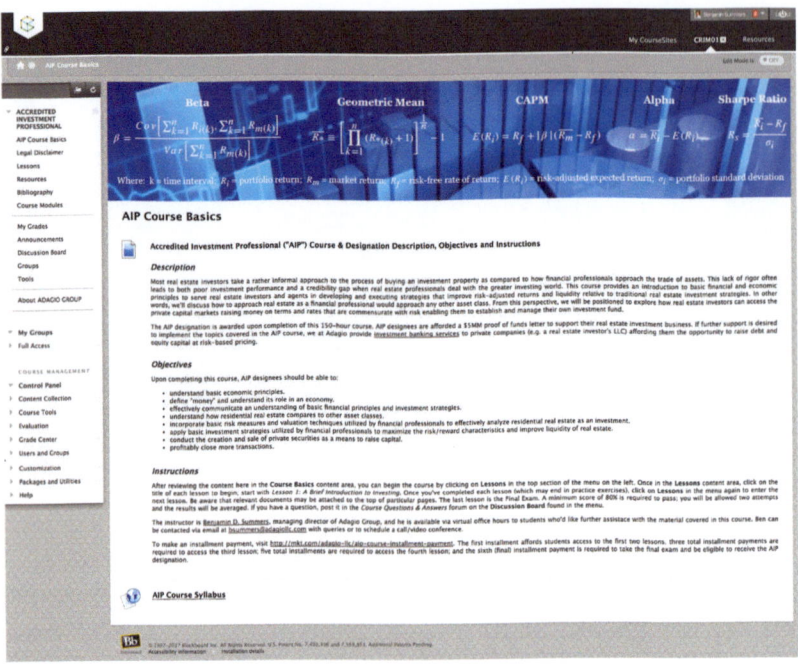

The Accredited Investment Professional Course Basics.

The AIP course covers much of what you'll find in the FINRA Series 65 exam manual except with much greater emphasis on private securities law, risk measures, and real estate as an asset class. The Series 65 doesn't really cover real estate, it doesn't say much on private securities law, and it's got nothing substantive on risk-adjusted performance analysis. The Kaplan Series 65 exam manual is about 800 pages, but there are maybe two pages that cover private securities law and one that covers REITs. The little mention that's given to risk-adjusted performance measures includes no calculations anywhere. It's no wonder why trying to distribute private structured products through investment advisers can be such a challenge. The AIP course does not go into great depth on publicly-traded securities and adviser compliance, but it does cover enough so that you can compete with publicly-traded assets and distribute through traditional channels.

The masterclass is all me for two and a half hours, but the AIP course provides additional perspective and valuable color to the text with videos from reputable real estate, finance, and legal experts to make the topics a little more clear and easier for you to grasp. It covers all of the components of investment banking and fund management that you need:

- Learn many of the investment adviser (Series 65) exam topics with an emphasis on private securities law and real estate as an asset class
- Learn from the most reputable financial and legal experts in the industry
- Learn the secrets of investment banking
- Learn exactly what money is, where it comes from, and how all forms are created
- Learn to convert your investing efforts into an asset you can sell
- Learn to create quality investment assets from thin air
- Learn what other types of investments you're competing against, their role in the market, and how to beat them
- Learn how to have people begging you to take their money.
- Learn to build wealth just like a bank, which represents the real shift in mindset for most people.

Here's the content of the AIP course:

Course Outline

1. Introduction to the Art & Science of Investing
    1.1. Investments & Finance
    1.2. What Is Economics?
        1.2.1. Classical Economics
        1.2.2. Keynesian Economics
        1.2.3. Austrian Economics
    1.3. How an Economy Grows and Why It Crashes by Peter Schiff
2. Money, Banking & Economics
    2.1. Types of Money
        2.1.1. Hard Money
        2.1.2. Fiat Money
    2.2. U.S. Dollar - A Brief History
    2.3. The Federal Reserve System
    2.4. Tools of The Fed
        2.4.1. Open Market Operations
            2.4.1.1. Quantitative Easing
            2.4.1.2. Operation Twist
        2.4.2. Reserve Requirements
        2.4.3. Discount Window
    2.5. Fractional Reserve Banking
    2.6. Measures of Money
        2.6.1. Money Supply
        2.6.2. M0, MB, M1, M2, M3, MZM
    2.7. Inflation
    2.8. Other Major Central Banks of the World
    2.9. The BIS, IMF & World Bank
    2.10. BRICS Nations, Theory & Bank
    2.11. Money & Economic Cycles
    2.12. Lesson 2 Practice Exercises
3. Asset Classes, Derivatives & Their Markets
    3.1. Assets & Liabilities
        3.1.1. Asset
        3.1.2. Liability
        3.1.3. Equity
    3.2. Introduction to Businesses
        3.2.1. Sole Proprietorships
        3.2.2. General Partnerships
        3.2.3. Limited Partnerships
        3.2.4. Limited Liability Companies

- 3.2.5. S Corporations
- 3.2.6. C Corporations
- 3.2.7. Financial Statements
- 3.3. What Is an Asset Class?
- 3.4. What Is a Market?
  - 3.4.1. Supply
  - 3.4.2. Demand
  - 3.4.3. Price
- 3.5. Securities
- 3.6. Traditional Assets
  - 3.6.1. Equities
  - 3.6.2. Fixed-Income
  - 3.6.3. Cash Equivalents
- 3.7. Liquid Assets
- 3.8. Currencies & Their Trade - FOREX
- 3.9. Money Markets
- 3.10. Bonds & The Bond Market
- 3.11. Stocks & The Stock Market
- 3.12. Investment Companies
  - 3.12.1. Mutual Fund
  - 3.12.2. Closed-End Fund
  - 3.12.3. Unit Investment Trust
  - 3.12.4. Private Investment Company
- 3.13. Exchange-Traded Funds
- 3.14. Real Estate Investment Trusts
- 3.15. Alternatives Assets
- 3.16. Hedge Funds
- 3.17. Private Equity
- 3.18. Venture Capital
- 3.19. Commodities
- 3.20. Derivatives
  - 3.20.1. Futures Contract
  - 3.20.2. Forward Contract
  - 3.20.3. Swap
  - 3.20.4. Call Option
  - 3.20.5. Put Option
  - 3.20.6. Straddle
  - 3.20.7. Short Sale
  - 3.20.8. Structured Finance
- 3.21. Futures Markets

- 3.22. Over-The-Counter Markets
- 3.23. Clearing Houses
- 3.24. Annuities
- 3.25. Life Insurance
- 3.26. Becoming Your Own Bank by R. Nelson Nash
- 3.27. Real Estate
  - 3.27.1. Residential Real Estate
  - 3.27.2. Commercial Real Estate
- 3.28. Brokered Markets
  - 3.28.1. Bid-Ask Spread
  - 3.28.2. Market Maker
  - 3.28.3. Securities Brokerage
  - 3.28.4. Business & Real Estate Brokerage
- 3.29. Lesson 3 Practice Exercises

4. Real Estate Finance
  - 4.1. Measuring Risk
    - 4.1.1. Capital Asset Pricing Model
    - 4.1.2. Sharpe Ratio
    - 4.1.3. Value at Risk
    - 4.1.4. Tail Risk
    - 4.1.5. The Black Swan
    - 4.1.6. Risk and Financial Professionals
    - 4.1.7. The Case of the Two and a Half Billion Percent Return
  - 4.2. Asset Valuation
    - 4.2.1. Intrinsic Value
    - 4.2.2. Current Market Value & Momentum
  - 4.3. Residential Real Estate vs. Other Asset Classes
    - 4.3.1. U.S. House Prices vs. Owner Equivalent Rent
    - 4.3.2. S&P 500
    - 4.3.3. Gold & Silver
  - 4.4. Real Estate Appraisal
    - 4.4.1. Sales Comparison Approach
    - 4.4.2. Income Capitalization Approach
    - 4.4.3. Cost Approach
  - 4.5. Analyzing Residential Real Estate
  - 4.6. Financing Structures in Real Estate

- 4.6.1. Working with Attorneys & Title Companies
- 4.6.2. Sale and Purchase Agreement
- 4.6.3. Contract for Deed
- 4.6.4. Mortgage Loans
- 4.6.5. Leases
- 4.6.6. Options
- 4.6.7. Swaps
7. Debt Service Coverage Ratio & Loan Constant
8. Real Estate Investment Strategies
    - 4.8.1. Opportunity Cost
    - 4.8.2. Long and Short Positions
    - 4.8.3. Long Positions in Real Estate
    - 4.8.4. Short Positions in Real Estate
    - 4.8.5. Holding a Portfolio vs. Flipping
    - 4.8.6. Debt vs. Equity
    - 4.8.7. The Role of Leverage
    - 4.8.8. Growing the Market for Real Estate Derivatives
9. Executing Real Estate Finance
    - 4.9.1. Using Financing Structures to Meet Investors' Goals
    - 4.9.2. Attracting Quality Investments with Debt
    - 4.9.3. Real Estate Development
    - 4.9.4. Sourcing & Negotiating with Sellers
        - 4.9.4.1. Wholesalers
        - 4.9.4.2. Rehabbers
        - 4.9.4.3. Contract Contingencies
        - 4.9.4.4. Creating a Discount Through Renegotiation
    - 4.9.5. Insurance Considerations
10. Raising Capital
    - 4.10.1. Introduction to Raising Capital
    - 4.10.2. Using Partners as a Source of Capital - Syndication & Funds
    - 4.10.3. Regulation D
    - 4.10.4. Investment Company Act of 1940 §3(c)
    - 4.10.5. Marketing & Compliance Documents
    - 4.10.6. Crowdfunding
    - 4.10.7. Investment Clubs
    - 4.10.8. Sourcing Buyers/Investors
    - 4.10.9. EB-5 Visa Program
11. Working with Financial Professionals
    - 4.11.1. Financial Planners, Registered Investment Advisors, et al
    - 4.11.2. Limited-Investment Securities & Insurance Brokers
    - 4.11.3. Investment Banks
    - 4.11.4. Hedge Funds
    - 4.11.5. Third-Party Marketers

- 4.11.6. Self-Directed IRAs
- 4.11.7. Mortgage Brokers
- 4.12. Tax Considerations
  - 4.12.1. Working with Tax Professionals
  - 4.12.2. Property Tax
  - 4.12.3. Depreciation
  - 4.12.4. Capital Gains Considerations
  - 4.12.5. 1031 Exchange
- 4.13. Building an Investment Team
  - 4.13.1. Appraisers
  - 4.13.2. Inspectors
  - 4.13.3. Contractors & Handymen
  - 4.13.4. Attorneys & Title Companies
  - 4.13.5. Tax Professionals
    - 4.13.5.1. CPAs
    - 4.13.5.2. 1031 Exchange Qualified Intermediaries
  - 4.13.6. Financial Professionals
    - 4.13.6.1. Financial Sales
    - 4.13.6.2. Insurance Agents & Adjusters
    - 4.13.6.3. Mortgage Brokers
  - 4.13.7. Social Media
    - 4.13.7.1. LinkedIn
- 4.14. Real Estate Agency (Florida)
  - 4.14.1. Buyer's Agency Agreement
  - 4.14.2. Compensation
- 4.15. Florida Land Trust
- 4.16. Lesson 4 Practice Exercises

5. Final Exam
   - 5.1. Scenario 1 Test
   - 5.2. Scenario 2 Test
   - 5.3. Scenario 3 Test
   - 5.4. Scenario 4 Test

Again, you can go through it sequentially, or you can use it as a reference for specific topics as you need them. Regardless of how you choose to use it,

- Syndicators and fund managers will be able to reduce their legal bills by thousands of dollars.

- Real estate investors will be able to reduce their capital outlay for acquisitions by thousands and even millions of dollars.

- Good financial advisors and capital aggregators will be able to eliminate thousands of dollars in waste from their marketing budgets and grow their AUM by millions of dollars with substantiated and differentiated messaging and product offerings.

- Real estate asset managers can eliminate their dependence on qualifying for mortgage loans.

- Retail investors will be able to save tens to hundreds of thousands of dollars in fees charged by ineffectual financial advisors and mediocre mutual funds, not to mention the reduced losses and increase in portfolio gains they'll see.

In short, the course is designed to help you implement all three of the shadow banking secrets we covered.

Remember, we charge hundreds of thousands and even millions of dollars to teach and implement this information on our clients' behalf. You could pay other expensive professionals to provide you bits and pieces of what's included here, but for much of it, there simply is no amount of money that could be thrown at anyone else to solve these problems.

How much is it worth to know you're protected from the next market crisis? How much is it worth to be able to start executing a new investment model and replace having no experience with a marketable theoretical track record? Where else could you possibly go to learn this or have it done for you? Where else could you go to become an authoritative creator of institutional-grade financial products? You can't even get that with an Ivy League MBA or the CFA designation.

What would it be worth to be able to sleep at night knowing your life savings is in a place where you don't have to be in constant worry about the markets? I guarantee, if there were another place to go for that kind of peace of mind, you'd be there already.

Valuation & Analysis Templates

One basic tool I've included that admittedly isn't too rare is a mortgage amortization schedule. It's probably worth noting that it's not just useful for amortizing mortgage loans, but I find it helpful when amortizing any expense or loan.

I've also included an income analysis template designed to value assets from purely an income perspective. This is obviously helpful if you've based your investment model on the income of any given asset such as a residential property as we discussed earlier. Of course, it outputs values such as return on equity, cash flow and break-even analyses, and scenario comparisons—and it's fully editable. Commercial real estate people likely have something similar, but this offers a slightly different and valuable perspective.

Real Property Deal Analysis Inputs
Property: XXXXXXXX

Deal Costs & Expenses	Scenario 1	Scenario 2	
Offer Price	$1,370,000	$1,370,000	
Down Payment %	50.00%	50.00%	
Mortgage Amount	$685,000	$685,000	
Closing Costs	$41,100	$41,100	
Loan Period (in years)	30	30	
Years until Balloon Due	5	4	
Interest Rate (if fixed)			
Unhide below rows if variable			
Year 1	4.50%	4.50%	
Year 2	6.50%	6.50%	
Year 3	6.50%	6.50%	
Year 4	6.50%	6.50%	
Year 5	8.50%		
Year 6			
Year 7			
Year 8			
Year 9			
Year 10			
Operating/Ownership Expenses			
Rental Mgmt Exp. (as %)	20%	20%	
Rental Mgmt Exp. (as $)	$9,790	$9,790	
HOA Fees			
Monthly	$604	$604	
Annual	$7,248	$7,248	
Property Tax			
Tax Rate %	1.06%	1.06%	
Annual Taxes Due	$14,522	$14,522	
Utilities			
Assumed avg mthly cost	$489	$489	
Annual	$5,868	$5,868	
Insurance %	0.00%	0.00%	0.00%
	$	$	$
Projected Increase in Occ Rate (as %)	11.00%	11.00%	
Projected Increase in Occ Rate (as $)	$6,050	$6,050	
Expected Income			
Expected Rental			
Peak Weekly	$3,800	$3,800	
No. of Wks Occ.*	20	20	
Total Wkly	$76,000	$76,000	

Real Property Deal Analysis Template inputs sheet.

APPLYING THE THREE SECRETS & TAILORED SOLUTIONS

XXXXXXXX							
Upfront Out of Pocket Cost ($726,100)	Initial Total Costs		Amount: $685,000	Loan Terms If fixed:	0.00%		
	Price ########		Amort. Per.	Year 1	4.50%		
	Closing Costs ($41,100)		Years 30	Year 2	6.50%		
Cap Rate 1.89%	Down Payment Amt:		Mos. 360	Year 3	6.50%		
	50.00% ($685,000)			Year 4	6.50%		
	Mtg Amt $685,000		*Duration in Mos. 60*	Year 5	8.50%		
				Year 6			
			Balloon Am ########	Year 7			
				Year 8			
				Year 9			
			Months before balloon. If not applicable, then should equal "Mos."	Year 10			

CASH FLOW AND RETURN MODELS

	Year 1		Year 2		Year 3		Year 4		Year 5		Totals
	Annual	Monthly	Annual	Monthly	Annual	Monthly	Annual	Monthly	Annual	Monthly	
Purchase Costs	1	12	13	24	25	36	37	48	49	60	
Beginning Principal	$685,000		$673,949		$669,430		$661,016		$652,343		
Principal Paid In Period	($11,051)	($4,520)		($8,414)		($8,673)		($9,021)		($41,678)
Cumulative Principal	($11,051)		($15,570)		($23,984)		($32,657)		($41,678)		
Interest Paid in Period	($29,927)		($46,598)		($42,704)		($42,445)		($42,096)		($203,771)
Cumulative Interest	($30,599)		($86,665)		($128,341)		($167,890)		($205,717)		
Payment Check	($40,978)		($51,118)		($51,118)		($51,118)		($51,118)		
YE Principal Remaining:	$673,949		$669,430		$661,016		$652,343		$643,322		
Debt Service Int Rate:	4.50%	0.375%	6.50%	0.542%	6.50%	0.542%	6.50%	0.542%	6.50%	0.542%	
Payment Due	($40,978)	($3,415)	($51,118)	($4,260)	($51,118)	($4,260)	($51,118)	($4,260)	($51,118)	($4,260)	($245,449)
Amortized Closing Costs (Straightline)	($8,220)	($685)	($8,220)	($685)	($8,220)	($685)	($8,220)	($685)	($8,220)	($685)	($41,100)
TOTAL PURCHASE COSTS	($49,198)	($4,100)	($59,338)	($4,945)	($59,338)	($4,945)	($59,338)	($4,945)	($59,338)	($4,945)	($286,549)
Operating Expenses											
Property Taxes @: 1.06%	($14,522)	########	($14,522)	########	($14,522)	########	($14,522)	########	($14,522)	########	($72,610)
HOA	($7,248)	($604)	($7,248)	($604)	($7,248)	($604)	($7,248)	($604)	($7,248)	($604)	($36,240)
Utilities	($5,868)	($489)	($5,868)	($489)	($5,868)	($489)	($5,868)	($489)	($5,868)	($489)	($29,340)
Property Management Cost 20% 20%	($11,000)	($917)	($12,210)	($1,018)	($13,553)	($1,129)	($15,044)	($1,254)	($15,044)	($1,254)	($66,851)
Insurance @: 0.00% 0%	$0	$0	$0	$0	$0	$0	$0	$0	$0	$0	$0
TOTAL OPERATING EXPENSES	($38,638)	($3,220)	($39,848)	($3,321)	($41,191)	($3,433)	($42,682)	($3,557)	($42,682)	($3,557)	($205,041)
Total Expenses	($87,836)	($7,320)	($99,186)	($8,265)	($100,529)	($8,377)	($102,020)	($8,502)	($102,020)	($8,502)	($491,590)
Income (Proj Occ Rate:)	55%		61%		68%		68%		68%		
Projected Increase in Occ Rate			11%		11%		11%		11%		
Gross Rental Income	$55,000	$4,583	$61,050	$5,088	$67,766	$5,647	$75,220	$6,268	$75,220	$6,268	$334,255
Investment Results											
NET OPERATING INCOME	$16,362	$1,363	$21,202	$1,767	$26,574	$2,215	$32,538	$2,711	$32,538	$2,711	$129,214
CASH FLOW (Net Inc min Debt Serv)	($24,616)	($2,051)	($29,916)	($2,493)	($24,543)	($2,045)	($18,580)	($1,548)	($18,580)	($1,548)	($116,235)
including Amort. Closing Costs	($32,836)	($2,736)	($38,136)	($3,178)	($32,763)	($2,730)	($26,800)	($2,233)	($26,800)	($2,233)	($157,335)
BREAKEVEN ANALYSIS											
Simple Breakeven											
Net Operating Income	$16,362		$37,564		$64,138		$96,676		$129,214		
Interest Paid on Loan	($30,599)		($86,665)		($128,341)		($167,890)		($205,717)		
Closing Costs (Not Amortized)	($41,100)		($41,100)		($41,100)		($41,100)		($41,100)		
Total	($55,337)		($90,201)		($105,303)		($112,314)		($117,603)		
BREAKEVEN PRICE	########		########		########		########		########		
Breakeven App. (As % of Purch Price)	4.0%		6.6%		7.7%		8.2%		8.6%		
Closing and Commission Costs at Exit	$115,568		$118,395		$119,619		$102,836		$103,202		
Breakeven App. w/Commission	########		########		########		########		########		
As % of Purchase Price	12.5%		15.2%		16.4%		0.1%		0.4%		

Real Property Deal Analysis Template model output sheet.

For those focused on the residential space—single family to fourplex buildings—this income valuation template will help you determine the most you should be willing to put into any given property. This template captures vacancy-adjusted gross income as opposed to just raw gross income and allows you to set your target cap rate so you can determine what a responsible basis looks like. When you operate as a financial institution, you can let this output determine how much to invest in a property as opposed to subjecting yourself to market cap rates as most investors do.

ADAGIO GROUP

INCOME APPROACH TO VALUE

SUBJECT PROPERTY

Address	123 ABC Street, Miami, FL 33139		
Purchase Price	$ 500,000	Square Footage	2,000
Property Type	SFR	Class	A
Target Cap Rate	4.00%	NOI Multiple	25.0

COMPARABLE INCOME ANALYSIS (Currently Rented)

Address	124 ABC Street, Miami, FL 33139		
* Monthly Gross Inco $	3,500	Square Footage	2,000
Days on Market	30	Rent/Sq Ft	$ 1.75
Address	125 ABC Street, Miami, FL 33139		
* Monthly Gross Inco $	3,500	Square Footage	2,000
Days on Market	30	Rent/Sq Ft	$ 1.75
Address	126 ABC Street, Miami, FL 33139		
* Monthly Gross Inco $	3,500	Square Footage	2,000
Days on Market	30	Rent/Sq Ft	$ 1.75
Average Gross Incom $	3,500		
Average Days on Mar	30	Average Rent/Sq Ft	$ 1.75

PRO FORMA INCOME

Monthly Gross Incom $	3,500		
Annual Gross Income $	42,000		
		Vacancy Rate	8.2%
		Annual Collection Costs	$ -
Effective Gross Incon $	38,548		
		Annual Property Taxes	$ 10,000
		Annual Hazard Insurance	$ 5,000
		Annual HOA Fees	$ 3,000
		Annual Utilities	$ -
		Annual Property Management	$ 3,855
		Annual Maintenance	$ -
		Annual Reserves	$ 3,000
Net Operating Incom $	13,693		
		Deferred Maintenance	$ 5,000

INCOME-BASED VALUE

$ 337,329

Adjusted

Real Estate Income Valuation Template.

Adagio Client Case Study

I've also included a case study that explains from the cradle to the grave how one large multifamily operator, which happens to have been our first advisory client, went through just about every problem you could imagine and the plan we developed to get them back on track to compliantly raising $5 million per month. They ran through hundreds of thousands of dollars to solve their problems, and I'm providing you the solutions, step by step.

The Problem

- Turnkey multifamily operator in business for over ten years stabilized blighted properties for resale at market value
- All properties, their rehab and holding costs were financed entirely with debt raised from the public (both accredited and non-accredited investors (averaging 150% LTV at 15% rate of interest)
- Came to us with approximately $40 million in real estate assets under management (AUM)
- Stabilized assets had negative equity (they were upside down), and NOI did not cover debt service
- Under investigation by three state securities administrators and the SEC

The Result

- Ceased illegal capital raising efforts and negotiated a financial restructuring of the existing portfolio to become solvent
- Amended their valuation process to insulate their investment portfolio from market cycles
- Raised capital at a rate of $5 million/month through four funds

Just about any challenge you could possibly be facing in your business right now is addressed in this case study. It's like a roadmap for implementing the AIP course and reaching your goals.

Who Is This For

I expect that it might get confusing to determine where you fit into all this. There's money flowing in; there's money flowing out; there are investors running an investment business and investors who simply buy passive debt and equity instruments; investments are being created and distributed through widely varying channels; and meanwhile, real estate and financial services people use a completely different vernacular to describe similar ideas. I'm going to clear this up once and for all right here.

What I've been describing is the entire financial services industry and all its participants, which includes, literally, everybody. Every single individual on the planet participates in one way, shape, or form, whether they want to or not: those who stash cash under their mattress, every employee with a 401k, anyone who's ever borrowed money, real estate investors, financial advisors, and fund managers. The whole point of this is to thrust you from wherever you currently are to the top of the industry utilizing your specific skills and resources as an informed master of your financial domain.

Who can benefit from all this?

1. Alternative investment managers including hedge fund managers, real estate investors, asset managers, lenders, and syndicators, (new or seasoned) who want to protect their business from the next market crash and/or who want access to unlimited capital to execute their investment business on their own terms

2. Retail investors and savers (those who aren't financial experts, such as retirees) who have a nest egg from which they need to generate decent income or growth,

but who can't afford much risk exposure and who want to meaningfully improve their portfolio and/or replace their financial advisor

3. Financial professionals who want to scale their business and create competitive advantage by incorporating reliable, quantifiable investment risk measures and alternative assets that generate demonstrably superior risk-adjusted performance into their practice

4. Real estate agents who want to compliantly serve their investor-clients in search of returns that are not available via the MLS or CoStar, are in need of 1031 assets, prefer quality passive investment opportunities, and who want to develop a niche as *the* investment real estate consultant in their market

5. Independent insurance agents, IRA custodians, accountants, or attorneys who want to compliantly serve their clients in need of better investment options than what they are being offered by their financial advisors or otherwise have available through their retirement accounts

6. Marketers and relationships builders who want to serve and monetize their network by compliantly providing exclusive access to high-quality alternative investments (like top-performing hedge funds)

Anyone in any of these groups can start their own fund or fund of funds, anyone can form an investment club, and anyone can, at least indirectly, invest in someone else's fund. The question is simply which role are your skills, interests, and resources best suited for? Regardless, all of these roads lead to the same place: true financial independence.

Risk-Adjusted Performance Calculator

If I had to guess, I'd say that the area where most people need the most help is the math because the risk calculations can get pretty complicated. The first thing I did was to build all of the significant risk-adjusted performance calculations in Excel. Excel spreadsheets can be a little difficult to hand over to others without having things break, so I hired a developer to take every calculation and output from the Excel spreadsheet and convert it to a user-friendly web application that scrapes current market data and updates in real time. Because it's a web application, it works on any platform, Mac or Windows PC. I'm really proud of this. I don't know of anywhere else you can find these calculations automated in one application, especially with such a user-friendly interface.

I'm giving you access to the risk-adjusted performance calculator. It incorporates every significant risk-adjusted performance metric, including illiquidity premiums for private securities, so you can easily compare any assets—from Apple stock to hedge funds to an advisor's portfolio to individual real estate assets—in meaningful, objective, apples-to-apples terms.

You'll see these calculations in the AIP course, but you don't have to learn how to do them yourself. Just plug in your return numbers and—voilà—an instantaneous output of the risk-adjusted performance ranging from a simple color code to a breakdown of each component metric. Like I just mentioned, it even includes the illiquidity premium for private securities so you can compare institutional-grade private funds and structured products apples-to-apples with publicly traded assets.

As I emphasized earlier, a minimum of one complete market cycle of performance data must be evaluated to generate any meaningful quantitative measures of risk. It's for this reason that the risk-adjusted performance calculator requires the return data input to encompass 2007 or earlier.

I understand that many asset managers haven't been around that long, and that's where our theoretical track-record services could come in and prove invaluable for the newer firms and funds.

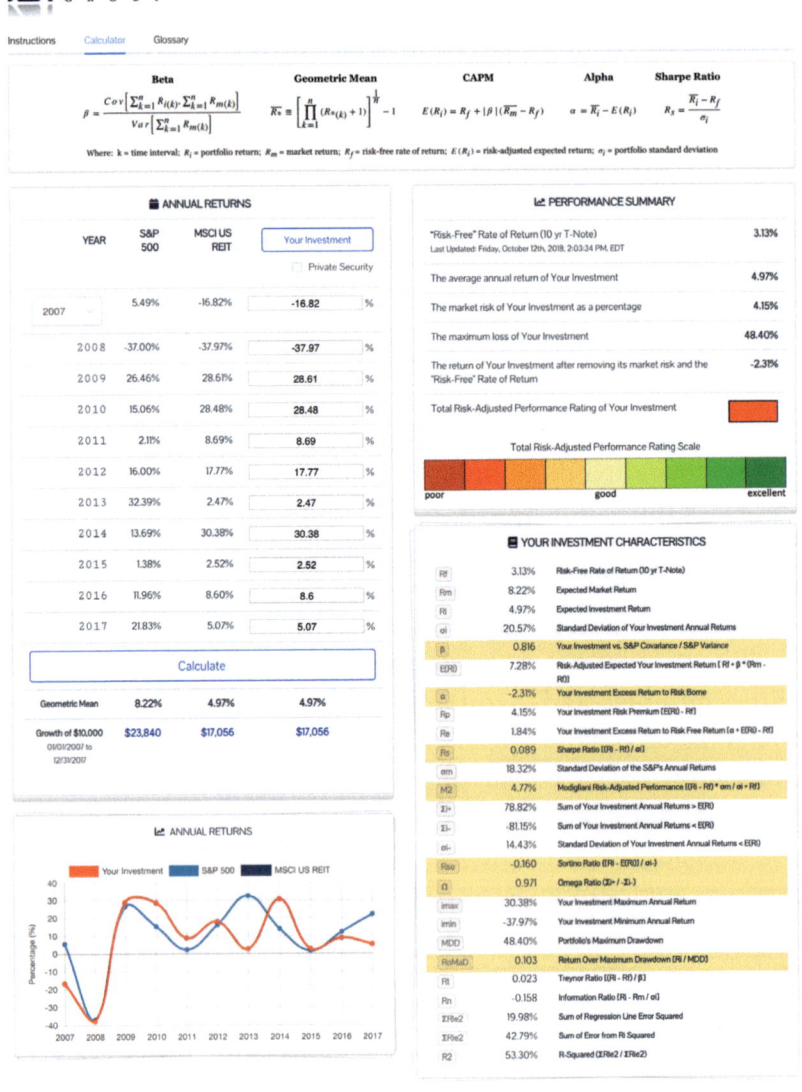

Risk-Adjusted Performance Calculator.

The risk-adjusted performance calculator is an essential tool. It cuts through the nonsense peddled by everyone from real estate syndicators to financial advisors to meaningfully measure investment quality in objective terms. You'll no longer be susceptible to the propaganda that governs the industry.

> CUT THROUGH THE PROPAGANDA AND SALESMANSHIP OF THE FINANCE AND REAL ESTATE INDUSTRIES TO ALWAYS CHOOSE THE BEST INVESTMENT BASED UPON MERIT.

It'll allow you to choose the best assets for building a portfolio, whether you're acquiring real estate or you're an investment adviser assembling assets for risk-conscious clients. Investment advisers and fund managers can also use it as a tool to objectively report the quality of their portfolios and communicate to their clients in clear, objective terms.

There is nothing like this available anywhere else, and it's a must-have for every serious investor and investment professional.

Sample Private Fund Documents

In addition to the "how" to operate an institutional-grade asset management business, you'll also need templates to guide you in creating corresponding institutional-grade documents.

We've paid hundreds of thousands of dollars to have marketing and offering documents drafted to a standard that would be respected by the biggest financial institutions in the world, and we're giving these templates to you. They include the two-pager, pitch book, offering memorandum, operating, and subscription agreements.

All you have to do is swap out any fund-specific information in the offering documents with that of your own. You'll want to have your docs reviewed by competent securities counsel to make sure everything is clearly consistent with your intent and compliant before you start distributing them, but not having to have these docs drafted from scratch will save you a great deal of money.

APPLYING THE THREE SECRETS & TAILORED SOLUTIONS

5100 Westheimer Rd • Ste 115
Houston, Texas 77056
Office: +1 (832) 356-0775
Fax: +1 (954) 229-2223
www.theadagiogroup.com

RESIDENTIAL INCOME ARBITRAGE   ADAGIO ABL, LLC

Investment Objective

Adagio ABL, LLC (the "Fund") is an open-end, residential income real estate fund focused on meeting the demand for non-recourse bridge financing in the investor market and is managed by Adagio, LLC (the "Manager"). The Fund utilizes low-LTV mortgages in conjunction with various lease and option structures designed to generate an internal hedge against residential real estate market (SFR & Multi-family) volatility via arbitrage.

Investment Approach

The Manager views residential real estate value as a function of its net rental income as opposed to the popular comparable sales model. Historically, while comparable sales values have experienced significant volatility, Owner Equivalent Rents ("OER"), as tracked by the U.S. Bureau of Labor Statistics ("BLS"), have been relatively stable. Constructing arbitrage trades between income-based and comparable sales valuations has insulated the Manager's portfolio from systemic risk, such as the crisis of 2008, while increasing overall returns.

Investment Composition & Attributes

Historically, the Manager's primary area of focus has been the residential income markets of Northwest Florida's (South Walton & Bay County) New Urban communities and the Tri-County area of South Florida (Miami-Dade, Broward, Palm Beach) because of their appeal as global destinations and abundance of investment opportunities. While these markets are beginning to peak, new opportunities remain in the markets of Tampa, FL, Jacksonville, FL, Pittsburgh, PA and Cleveland, OH based upon unique local factors. Across single family markets, comparable sales values begin to diverge from respective rental income at list prices of approximately $70k. The median property value of the Fund's portfolio is $194k with the average value being $260k; the Fund's corresponding median and mean bases are $124k and $171k, respectively. To offset risk associated with the illiquid nature of real estate assets and in anticipation of imminent market corrections, the Fund's portfolio of liquid securities will be further moved into cash and increase to above 25% of NAV from the 15% minimum.

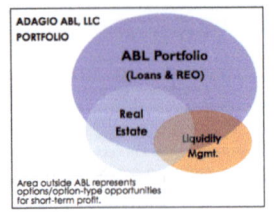

Terms for New Investments

For detailed investment terms, consult your Private Placement Memorandum or Adagio representative.

Manager AUM
$31 MM

Number of Investors
HNWI: 2
Other Private: 2
TOTAL: 4

AUM MILESTONE: $150MM
Gain full access to capital markets (significantly reducing cost of capital, i.e. low cost leverage) and begin institutionalizing ABL nationally via reverse mergers of residential "hard money" lenders.

Class A Membership Units ("Preferred Shares")
- Cumulative, Non-Convertible & Non-Participating
- Minimum Investment: $1,500,000 *
- Lock-Up: 60 months
- 7% Annual Preferred Return Paid as Quarterly Dividend

Class B Membership Units ("Common Shares")
- Minimum Investment: $1,500,000 *
- Lock-Up: 60 months
- Net 70/30 with 7% Threshold calculated against High-Water Mark

* Subject to waiver

Managing Principals

Benjamin D. Summers, *Managing Director & Founder*

Recognizing the strengths of real estate as an investment vehicle, Ben founded Adagio in 2005 on the unique investment strategies he developed to mitigate risk and capture value appreciation in the residential income market. In addition to real estate, Ben has significant senior management experience within the energy services sector managing large-scale infrastructure development projects in Africa and developing global markets for innovative drilling technologies. His move into the energy services arena was preceded by a professional baseball career begun via the San Diego Padres organization. Ben graduated from Louisiana State University with a Bachelor of Science degree in physics having studied music as a second discipline.

Joseph A. Maiullo IV, *Executive Director*

Joe has over nine years of Wall Street experience at firms including Morgan Stanley and UBS. In addition to his role at Adagio, Joe maintains his position at Morgan Stanley working closely with institutional clients and ultra high net worth families in coordinating investments across all asset classes, including alternative investments; additionally, Joe advises middle market institutional clients providing equity sales coverage. Joe graduated from Michigan State University with a Bachelor of Arts degree in interdisciplinary studies in economics.

Read "General Presentation Notes" at the end of this document for important disclosures.   Privileged, Confidential and Proprietary
Copyright © 2016 by Adagio, LLC

Adagio ABL Fact Card page 1.

THE SHADOW BANKER'S SECRETS PROGRAM

5100 Westheimer Rd • Ste 115
Houston, Texas 77056
Office: +1 (832) 356-0775
Fax: +1 (954) 229-2223
www.theadagiogroup.com

RESIDENTIAL INCOME ARBITRAGE   ADAGIO ABL, LLC

Annual Gross Performance

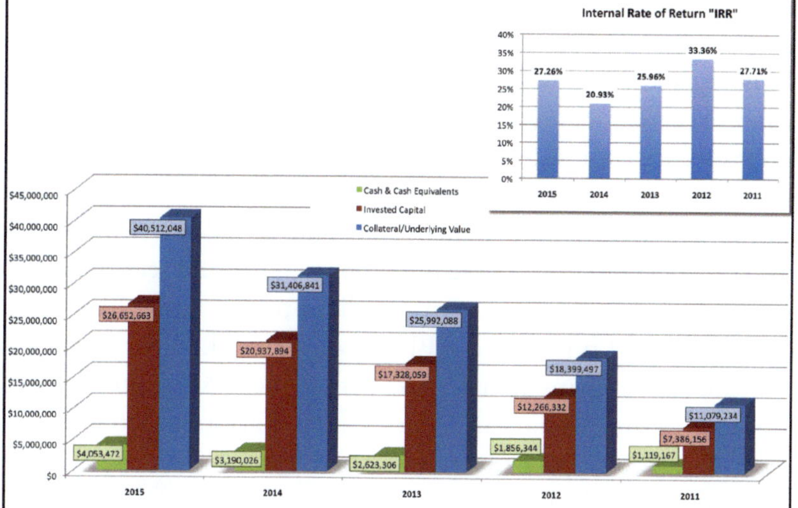

Internal Rate of Return "IRR"

Year	IRR
2015	27.26%
2014	20.93%
2013	25.96%
2012	33.36%
2011	27.71%

Year	Cash & Cash Equivalents	Invested Capital	Collateral/Underlying Value
2015	$4,053,472	$26,652,663	$40,512,048
2014	$3,190,026	$20,937,894	$31,406,841
2013	$2,623,306	$17,328,059	$25,992,088
2012	$1,856,344	$12,266,332	$18,399,497
2011	$1,119,167	$7,386,156	$11,079,234

Risk Characteristics (2007 to Present)

Capital Asset Pricing Model ("CAPM")
$E(Ri) = Rf + \beta*(Rm - Rf)$

ABL vs. S&P Covariance   0.00017
S&P Variance   0.0354

Sharpe Ratio
$Rs = (Ri - Rf) / \sigma$

Rf	2.27%	Risk Free Return (*10 yr T-Note as of 12/31/15*)
Rm	6.40%	Expected Market Return (*S&P Average Annual Return*)
Ri	28.94%	Expected Asset Return (*Asset Average Return*)
σ	5.91%	Standard Deviation of Adagio's Annual Returns
β	0.0048	ABL vs. S&P Covariance / S&P Variance
E(Ri)	2.29%	Risk Adjusted Expected ABL Return
α	26.65%	ABL Excess Return to Risk Borne
Rp	0.02%	Asset Risk Premium (*E(Ri) - Rf*)
Re	26.67%	Asset Excess Return to Risk Free Return (*σ + E(Ri) - Rf*)
Rs	4.511	Sharpe Ratio

Annual Returns

	ADAGIO ABL	S&P 500	MSCI US REIT Index
2007	26.32%	5.49%	-16.82%
2008	32.07%	-37.00%	-37.97%
2009	41.56%	26.46%	28.61%
2010	26.32%	15.06%	28.48%
2011	27.71%	2.11%	8.69%
2012	33.36%	16.00%	17.77%
2013	25.96%	32.39%	2.47%
2014	20.93%	13.69%	30.38%
2015	27.26%	1.38%	25.20%
Average *	28.94%	6.40%	6.92%

* Geometric Mean

Performance does not include Adagio management and performance fees ("Adagio Fees"). The Adagio Fees and any other expenses that the investor incurs will reduce the returns to investors. The Adagio Fees are described in the Private Placement Memorandum. Past performance is not indicative of future results. Full year and/or YTD performance may not equal the monthly or quarterly compounded results due to the effects of rounding and may include estimated and/or unaudited results.

Read "General Presentation Notes" at the end of this document for important disclosures.

Privileged, Confidential and Proprietary
Copyright © 2016 ADAGIO, LLC

Adagio ABL Fact Card page 2.

The good news is that when you do it right, you can presell your fund with the marketing documents before you pay to have your offering documents reviewed. This prevents you from unnecessarily spending money without first knowing whether you'll be able to sell shares in the fund.

You can use these documents to set up funds for your own investment model, or if your greatest asset lies in relationship building and you don't have an investment model of your own, you can use these documents to create a fund of funds that allows you to aggregate capital to invest with other quality asset managers.

When you've structured your business and investment model properly, the offering documents become actual assets with value in and of themselves. These documents are actual securities that are the private counterpart to publicly-traded assets like stock, bonds, mutual funds, and REITs. Let that sink in for a minute. You are able to print actual assets with value. Just like the Federal Reserve creates dollars in their system that are printed by the Treasury, you're able to create valuable securities that can be printed and sold in million-dollar-plus tranches.

Offering Documents

- Offering memorandum
- Fund operating agreement
- Subscription agreement

Marketing Documents

- Fact card
- Pitch book

Now the question becomes: how many assets are you able to print?

Federal Securities Laws and Forms

I also thought it would be helpful to aggregate all of the relevant securities laws in one convenient place for reference, so they're all aggregated within the resources section of the AIP course. You can look up any rule or regulation needed to guide compliant securities issuance and fund management all in one place.

- Securities Act of 1933
- Securities Exchange Act of 1934
- Investment Company Act of 1940
- Investment Advisors Act of 1940
- Dodd-Frank Act
- JOBS Act
- Uniform Securities Act
- State Securities Administrators
- SEC Rules & Regulations
- SEC No-Action Letters
- SEC Form D
- SEC Form ADV

5 One-Hour Private Consultations with Ben Summers ($975 Hourly Rate)

Benjamin D. Summers

Even with all that, I know that at some point you're still going to have questions. Each of you has different interests, skills, and resources and may want some guidance on applying everything at your disposal to develop an approach perfectly tailored for you. At this time, my billable rate is $975 an hour, but I'm going to give you five one-hour private phone consultations with me to help you through any sticking points you may come across and maximize your potential for success.

You'll probably want to save them until after you've gotten through all of the materials I've provided you first, but that's your call. They are yours to use whenever you'd like.

$5 Million Proof of Funds Letter
(issued by Adagio Group upon successful completion of the AIP course)

If you're just starting out, your theoretical track record will be very helpful, but it will also be helpful to have some money behind you. Upon successfully completing the AIP course, we'll provide you with a $5 million proof of funds letter to give you the strength and credibility to sit at the table with just about anyone. For real estate asset managers, it should go a long way to help you get just about any property you find under contract.

Our Offer

*	Masterclass on Investment Banking in Real Estate	$199 Value
*	Accredited Investment Professional ("AIP") Course & Designation	$4,995 Value
*	Amortization, Income Analysis & Valuation Templates	$250 Value
*	$5MM / Month Capital Raising Case Study	$150 Value
*	Risk-Adjusted Performance Calculator (1 Month Free Access)	$750 Value
*	Sample Private Fund & Investment Club Documents	$185,000 Value
*	Aggregated Federal Securities Laws & Forms	$100 Value
*	5 One-Hour Consultations with *Ben Summers*	$4,875 Value
*	$5MM Proof of Funds Letter	$5,000 Value
TOTAL VALUE		**$201,319**

The Shadow Banker's Secrets Program offer.

Is everything you need to scale your investment business by hundreds of millions of dollars worth $200,000?

Adagio's clients are putting up over $750,000 for us to implement these skills for them, plus millions on the backend.

It should be absolutely obvious by now that what we're offering is better than any other approach you could possibly imagine to raise money, grow AUM, and protect your portfolio from market crises. This is the way, and Adagio Institute was established to provide it to you.

Adagio Institute is a 501(c)3 public charity dedicated to financial education. Its purpose is to help the public navigate the propaganda of the financial services industry, to provide financial professionals who recognize the shortcomings of the industry an opportunity to do better, and to help deserving asset managers access the capital they need to scale their business responsibly. Subsidizing this offer is one of the most effective ways the institute can help fulfill its mission.

You can see why this package is well worth $200,000. The business of finance is just expensive… there's no way around it. But $200,000 is still out of reach for many deserving people.

That's why Adagio Institute was created—to provide access to exclusive financial knowledge and resources to as many people as possible. As a public charity, when we are able, we create packages that do just that and subsidize a vast majority of the cost.

I'm happy to announce that at this time, we are able to offer this entire package for only $6,725, and I feel really good about that.

GET STARTED FOR JUST
$6,725
Over 96% Off!

The Shadow Banker's Secrets Program discounted and guaranteed offer.

I'm so confident in what this package can do for you and eager to get these skills and resources out into the marketplace that if you sign up via the special link provided in this book, and if you're not satisfied for any reason, or if you decide that becoming your own bank is simply not for you, just let us know, and we'll refund your money.

The Shadow Banker's Secrets Program provides a 30-day money-back guarantee.

You have 30 days to go through everything and begin applying the materials. If at any time during that period you decide this pursuit is not for you, just let us know, and we'll get your money back to you. You can keep the templates and any other downloadable assets that are included. I don't know how to make the process any more accessible.

Get started now at www.adagioinstitute.org/sbs-program-order

We're a public charity, and the sole purpose of our existence is to help you, and by extension, the public-at-large.

One of the objections I often hear, even from some of the smartest and most driven people you're going to meet, is, "I'm just starting out, and I need more experience before I'm ready for this advanced stuff." If you are serious about investing, it's never too early to learn the fundamentals of professional finance. This is a quote from one of our clients that I think really drives the point home:

> *"Ben, if I had spoken to you twelve months ago, it would have been a lot easier. I thought that I wasn't ready for this "complicated stuff" and that understanding real estate investing and syndication was all I really needed. But the truth is that if I had started out running my investment business the right way, instead of thinking I needed to grow what I already had first, it would have been much easier to start accessing the capital I needed when I was ready. Now, I have to go back and rework all of the problems I didn't even know I was creating for myself. I'm just glad I have the chance to fix these problems before the market ruined my business."*

It's never too early to start doing things the right way.

As I mentioned earlier, this offer was structured specifically for those who aren't ready for us to take them on as a client yet. It provides almost everyone, no matter where they currently are in their journey, the opportunity to achieve absolute financial independence.

APPLYING THE THREE SECRETS & TAILORED SOLUTIONS

• Masterclass on Investment Banking in Real Estate	$199 Value	
• Accredited Investment Professional ("AIP") Course & Designation	$4,995 Value	
• Amortization, Income Analysis & Valuation Templates	$250 Value	
• $5MM / Month Capital Raising Case Study	$150 Value	
• Risk-Adjusted Performance Calculator (1 Month Free Access)	$750 Value	
• Sample Private Fund & Investment Club Documents	$185,000 Value	
• Aggregated Federal Securities Laws & Forms	$100 Value	
• 5 One-Hour Consultations with *Ben Summers*	$4,875 Value	
• $5MM Proof of Funds Letter	$5,000 Value	
TOTAL VALUE	**$201,319**	

GET STARTED TODAY FOR JUST

$6,725

Get Started Now at:
www.adagioinstitute.org/sbs-program-order

The Shadow Banker's Secrets Program discounted and guaranteed offer.

FAQs

"What else do I need?"

I've tried very hard to include everything you could possibly need. If you find that you need something that's not included, let me know, and I'll add it. I genuinely want you to be successful.

"Do you offer payment plans for The Shadow Banker's Secrets Program?"

No, but don't forget your credit card gives you some lead time to start making progress before you have to begin making payments.

"What if I can't afford The Shadow Banker's Secrets Program?"

If you think you can't afford this now, you need it more than anyone else. Poor people say they can't afford it and give up. Rich people say *how* can I afford it and commit to finding a way to make it happen. I've seen over and over again throughout my career that people who are given things for free don't value them. There's something that happens in the psychology of humans that motivates commitment when they're forced to pay for something. What you have to pay for all of the value included here practically makes it a steal. One of the quickest ways to afford the program is to become an affiliate. To learn more and register, visit www.adagioinstitute.org/affiliates.

"What's the difference between The Shadow Banker's Secrets Program and other real estate and capital raising programs?"

First, I'm a licensed financial professional, and compliance is at the forefront of everything we do. Second, this program is meant for all alternative asset managers and allocators who operate within any asset class, not just real estate. In terms of the unique value of this program, where else can you find this level of expertise in not only quantitative finance but also real estate, hedge funds, private equity, securities law, and financial product distribution? This program provides the means that financial institutions use to capitalize themselves, and there's simply nothing else like it. Real estate gurus teach you how to run a real estate business and maybe talk about how to ask friends and family for money. This program teaches you how to be the bank for those people.

"Where do I start?"

There is a lot to consider, and I get that it can feel overwhelming. That being said, this book is designed to solve that very problem. If you feel you need more assistance than what is provided in this book, follow the sections of the Shadow Banker's Secrets Program as it's laid out, and when you get stuck, use one of your five one-hour consultations with me to get over the hump.

Epilogue
THE THREE ECONOMIC ROLES

There are three economic roles that govern how we all do business: the consumer, the producer, and the banker. Understanding this dynamic will make you rethink your place in the economy and how you want to position yourself to earn money.

The three economic roles.

EPILOGUE: THE THREE ECONOMIC ROLES

The consumer provides labor to the producer. The producer creates and provides value that the consumer buys. The banker provides the producer money via debt and equity to operate his business. The banker also provides the consumer with money via interest-bearing loans to buy from the producer.

While the consumer is constrained by the time he has available to sell to the producer as labor, and the producer is constrained by the value he is able to create and provide the consumer, the banker is making money from both the producer and the consumer by providing them nothing more than money. And as I've spent this entire book discussing, the banker is effectively able to create that money from thin air.

The consumer lives his entire economic life as a servant to the producer. He chooses what to learn and how to spend his time almost entirely based upon the demands of the producer. The producer has to create real, tangible value that consumers are willing to buy. This is a high-risk, capital-intensive effort.

Meanwhile, the banker makes money simply by providing money to the producer and the consumer.

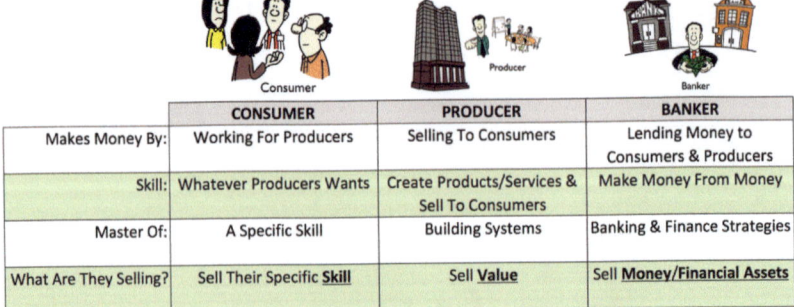

The characteristics of the three economic roles.

What expertise must each of these have to fulfill their roles? The consumer has to master the specific skill that's in demand by the producer. The producer must be a master of building systems that can produce value in an economically viable way. And the banker must be a master of banking and financial strategies, the very expertise I'm providing you.

What are they selling? The consumer sells their specific skill by the hour; they're literally selling away their lives. The producer is selling value. And the banker is selling money and other financial assets that they themselves are able to create and scale from nothing more than their expertise.

This dynamic between the three economic roles was eloquently summarized in an epigram quoted in John C. Bogle's book, *Enough*:

> "Some men wrest [make] a living from nature; this is called work. [CONSUMERS]
>
> Some men wrest a living from those who wrest a living from nature; this is called trade. [PRODUCERS]
>
> Some men wrest a living from those who wrest a living from those who wrest a living from nature; this is called finance." [BANKERS]

This is the nature of mankind. Every social reset in history has defaulted back to this dynamic. If these are the three options we have to choose from, which one do you want for yourself?

If you haven't chosen to be the bank by now, how much of your life will you continue to choose to give up to those who have? You're not just giving up money, but you're forfeiting your time, your value, and ultimately, control over your own destiny.

Appendix
Questions and Answers

HOW TO TAKE ADVANTAGE OF OUR DEBT-BACKED CURRENCY

Interviewer: How should the retail and consumer channels use the knowledge that our money supply is actually tied to the total amount of bank-issued debt versus the total value of goods and services?

Ben Summers: I don't know that there's a whole lot that can be done specifically in terms of managing that relationship. The popular answer is to escape to gold or real estate, but people forget that time is one of the most important variables in finance. Just because the fundamentals imply a certain value today, that doesn't mean the "true" value will be expressed any time soon. As the adage goes, "The market can remain irrational longer than you can stay solvent." We've seen gold interests get crushed for the past ten years, and that's not an indictment against the intrinsic value of gold—it's simply an example of how unpredictable markets can be, and that timing is very important.

It's not a simple answer, and I think that's an important point to drive home.

There are things you can do. For example, private lending via a convertible fixed-income structure against real estate is a great strategy, but that's a business in and of itself, and it takes a degree of expertise to structure and execute properly. For example, people have to understand how to value real estate through the lens of net operating income. Judicial foreclosure in foreclosure states can severely delay and consume the return on your investment if it's not properly managed. There is a myriad of considerations that must be taken into account with the appropriate level of expertise to be successful.

The idea here is to express that yes, there are fundamental, structural problems with the nature of our currency, and there are things that can be done, but they're not simple. I would like to motivate a deeper dive for those who actually care. I would expect that everyone should care. Whether you're interested in saving the whales, hugging trees, or making money, money itself is the driver of any initiative that you want to see through to fruition. You simply can't be effective without money, whether it's your money or somebody else's.

For example, people know about the work of Mother Teresa because there were a lot of media dollars that told her stories over the years, not to mention the financial backing of the Catholic Church to promote her story. I promise you that there are a lot of people in the world just as selfless as her that you'll never know about whose causes have been lost. No matter what you want to pursue in life, you need money to do it—typically a lot. Those who tell you money is bad or not important are either stupid are con artists—often both.

The reason I say that I want to motivate people to take a deeper dive is that 99% of the people I come across who are aware of these things—and I mean the deep-seated corruption by the banking cartel—throw up their hands and say, "There's nothing that can be done, so why bother?" That's not true, and I'm a testament to that.

This entire book is an effort to provide the what and how in response to these issues, and it's effective. Granted,

I'm not necessarily providing the solution to overthrow the oligarchy, but I am providing the solutions to escape its shackles and achieve true and absolute freedom, which starts with real financial expertise. And by financial expertise, I'm not talking about Suze Orman or FINRA-sanctioned materials.

Finance is the most sophisticated business in the economy. Its corruption and dysfunction are the most metastatic, pervasive, and complex problems that the world faces. That is not an exaggeration. We're talking about the biggest possible problems all stemming from this one complex industry that effectively rules all others.

The first step to do something about it is to understand the roles in the finance industry and the tools they use to secure their power. It's not just complexity for the sake of being complex. Effectively holding the entire world as debt-serfs and extracting trillions of dollars from the entire globe's real productivity requires an evolution into complexity. People have to have some cursory level of understanding of this complexity before they can begin to address the problem or navigate it. It all starts with an understanding of the repercussions of being dependent upon debt-backed currency.

You can sort of take two paths as you read this book. You can either use this information as a means to evaluate professionals who are sufficiently sophisticated to navigate this climate and solve these problems on your behalf, or you can dive even further and attempt to solve these problems on your own.

WHAT WOULD RESULT FROM AN ASSET-BACKED CURRENCY

Interviewer: If we went back to an asset-backed currency, would that impede our ability to grow as an economy? Could it potentially hurt the average person as things trickle down?

Ben Summers: In short, no. The big takeaway is that debt-based currency facilitates the financialization of an economy. An asset-based currency does not stifle growth, but it does prevent bubbles to an extent. It prevents irrational, misguided growth because people have to put up real assets to finance it. A central bank can't control interest rates as a means to incentivize people to allocate to things they wouldn't otherwise. It doesn't allow for excessive leverage. Growth is more responsible, it's more stable, and it's predicated on real production—at least it should be—anything can be manipulated. But if it's run properly, it's predicated on real, tangible development and production of goods and services, not financial manipulation.

I can securitize all sorts of stuff. In the most basic example of a fund, the money comes from retail investors who have cash and want to invest it somewhere to grow. The operator who's being funded doesn't have any money; all he has is an idea. If he doesn't get the money, it will remain an idea, and an idea alone doesn't have any real value. But, when I can securitize that idea—to maintain the theme, I'll issue debt securities in this example—then what happens is a retail investor buys that debt instrument. The money from that purchase goes to finance the operator. Now, he has money in his account to run his business, and the retail investor has the equivalent amount of money in his savings account in the form of securities. Now, in this case, it's not technically a savings account. It can be a brokerage account or whatever type of ledger is used to keep track of investments. The point is that both balance sheets show the same amount of money. The retail investor doesn't report that they donated that money. He still shows that balance in his account, and it is a growing balance. The real estate operator also has that same balance, so we've effectively doubled the money with the stroke of a pen. Now, that's not a perfect example, because that's not fractional reserve banking, but that's an example of how money grows through financialization.

Now, when you have unfettered debt creation that is even less secured, then that scenario can explode. In the case that I just described, I am constrained by the amount of quality deal flow I generate and responsibly allocate to that produces growth in value. In central and fractional reserve banking, the system doesn't actually need real value to back the creation of new money. Retail banks can borrow from the Federal Reserve System, effectively unfettered. They have some minimum asset requirements, but they can lever it up. The base currency gets multiplied by a factor of the inverse reserve ratio. It's not constrained by real value creation but simply by an arbitrary reserve ratio set by the Fed and people's willingness to borrow.

The Federal Reserve System is an independent entity from Congress and from the Executive Branch. It has unchecked ability to issue currency and to dictate the rate at which it multiplies. The rate at which it multiplies is not based upon any material grassroots fundamentals, like it was in Canada, pre-1935. It's based upon the arbitrary decisions of a Federal Reserve Board and their prognosticators, who have little to no ability to predict the future as has been demonstrated over and over again.

When you look at the material products of the finance industry, versus the material products of a grocer or a technology company, that should say something in and of itself. In other words, values are not based on fundamental, real things. They're based upon an artificially propped-up monetary policy that is governed by economists with a conflict of interests, attempting to predict the future with a bias toward predicting the future in a way that supports their and their cronies' interests. They have the power to support arbitrary values across the board, around the world, which makes it impossible to consistently and reliably invest based upon fundamentals. This undermines the simple solution that is, "Just buy real estate, just buy gold." They've been suppressing the price of gold for 10 years now. The London Bullion

Exchange, just a few years ago, was caught manipulating precious metal prices.

The market capitalization of Apple, the value of that company, the value of the aggregate of its share prices, is greater than the current face value of all the gold stores in the world. What does that tell you? What would you rather have? Would you rather own Apple or all the gold in the world?

WHAT WILL THE NEXT CRISIS LOOK LIKE

Interviewer: That's actually a great segue into the next question. So, we've established that our bank-issued debt-backed currency is effectively a Ponzi scheme that will inevitably collapse, but what will that resulting collapse look like, and how will it affect the average citizen as compared to previous financial crises?

Ben Summers: Yes. There's a common theme that each crisis is consistently bigger than the last one. The Fed doesn't let the economy correct itself and recover, letting assets and resources be allocated to the places where they'd be best served, which causes short-term pain while things shift back to where they need to be. Instead, the Fed invariably stimulates the economy, injecting more money in the very place that shouldn't have had it to begin with—propping up the economic imbalance even higher than it was before. When it blows up next time, you're re-blowing up the original problem plus the increased problem that you exacerbated. And that just continues to build, and the inherent risk becomes more fundamentally systematic with each bailout or stimulus package, whether that's artificially reducing interest rates through QE or whatever. Now, the Fed has backed itself into a corner with artificially low interest rates it can never raise without blowing up the entire economy and itself in the process.

The next crisis will be bigger than the last one. Here's the problem—and this goes back to the point that I made earlier—some people did well in the 2008 financial crisis and are expecting it to occur again because the fundamentals point in that direction, but the power of the financial industry is global. It is the top of the pyramid. They control almost everything, to the extent that they can. So, they're not just going to let everything blow up. They are doing everything they can to protect this house of cards, and it's not just printing money.

It's also strategic wars to prevent people from ditching certain currencies. It's a comprehensive effort. Loosely speaking, the U.S. is the military arm of the Federal Reserve to enforce its policies globally. That's a whole separate geopolitical discussion that we're not going to dive into, but it's not just a matter of printing money. It's a matter of having enforcers to make sure that everything doesn't fall apart. Again, that power is global, and it's oligarchical. Things aren't just going to fall apart because they look bad. The most powerful force in the world is fighting to maintain it.

What that means is it's impossible to predict when and how everything is going to blow up. There are a lot of competent financial people who understood this stuff and who did well—not a lot, but a few that did well in 2008, 2009—but have lost their ass since then because they've continued to bet on the fundamentals, and the fundamentals have been buried by manipulation for the past ten years—hell, really for the last 50 years going back to 1971. Timing is everything in finance.

One example of betting on the fundamentals would be shorting the bond market. When it blows up, you're going to be rich, but while it's going up, you're losing your ass and eventually, you're going to run out of money or people are going to call you on it, and you'll be bankrupt. The banking cartel knows this; they have a pulse on the investing attitude of the public, and they're able to manipulate prices in a way to keep people from making what you might call simple bets to navigate a climate. Again, and this point cannot be emphasized enough, understanding fundamentals alone is not enough.

Timing is where it's at, and no one can predict when or how the next crisis will occur. I expect it will occur under cover of some large war or huge civil unrest, and then everybody will say, "See, it's because of the war, or it's because of the civil unrest; that's why the market blew up." That will be the cover for the fundamentals to distract the people from the true culprit, the banking system. You can see it being orchestrated now through the media. They're certainly not spurring critical thinking and civil conversation about these fundamental issues: the nature of the national debt, the Fed's balance sheet, the effects of central and fractional reserve banking. The news has devolved into unveiled biased editorial that is obviously fomenting increasing polarization throughout the country around simplistic red herrings. How do you think that ends? With intellectual debate amongst the populace and a civil resolution to agree to disagree?

Here's one more point that's worth noting that makes this more tangible and less abstract. Let's say you read the prologue of this book in 2011 and said, "I know that the currency of the United States is artificially inflated, and I know that gold has real, intrinsic value. It has for thousands of years. I'm 70 years old; I'm retiring five years late, and I'm going to buy gold because I know the financial markets are messed up; and I'll be safe there."

Gold bottomed in late 2015, and if you bought gold in 2011 when it seemed prudent, you would have lost a lot of your retirement savings. Furthermore, gold does not provide any dividend. It doesn't pay you a monthly income to live off of. You can be right; you can say, "I recognize the fundamentals," but it's a manipulated market. So, now you're 75 years old and the value of your retirement portfolio lost about 40% minus what you had to withdraw to live off of because it generated no income for you. What do you do? There's nothing to say it won't go down for another 10 years or stay the same for 10 years. You'd have been better off just holding cash under your mattress, which is a fiat currency with no fundamental value, so what do you do? It's not a simple answer.

HOW TO PROTECT YOURSELF FROM ECONOMIC COLLAPSE

Interviewer: Is there a way to protect ourselves financially from this collapse that's going to happen?

Ben Summers: There are ways, but let's first dive into a couple of generalities. Number one, private assets versus public assets. Public assets, stocks and bonds, mutual funds—stuff that your financial advisor pushes on you—those types of investments are the most susceptible to manipulation and generally experience the greatest market risk, and those markets are most efficient. What that means is they're probably the worst, and the reason they're probably the worst is that there's the greatest potential for a disconnect between the fundamental value of those assets and the market price of those assets.

One example would be to look at Caterpillar in 2008. Caterpillar, a manufacturing company, had physical inventory that had real value. They owned tractors and trucks, and the price of those trucks and tractors didn't really change. The change was the rate at which they were purchased. What happened is that companies like Caterpillar that owned physical, tangible assets with real, measurable value, were valued on the stock market at less than the sum of the value of their assets alone, not to mention the intangible value of the company: the marketing, the executive expertise, etc. There was nothing you could do about that. You could whine, you could cry, you could say, "I own such and such company, and it has a billion dollars in cash in the bank. It's not fair that it's only selling for $900 million right now." But there was nothing you could do about it. What was going on? There was a complete disconnect because the market was bad and lacked liquidity, so it dictated the aggregate value of the company was worth less than the sum of its parts.

It's called the secondary market where publicly-traded stocks and bonds are sold. The value of the shares in a company on the secondary market was very much disconnected from the fundamental value. That's what's easily manipulated by monetary policy, for example.

How do you know if your investments are safe? How do you know they won't randomly dive in value because of public sentiment or whatever? You don't.

One of the first places to look is private alternative assets (which means they are not publicly traded). There's an entire lesson within the Accredited Investment Professional course dedicated to the various asset classes and the differences between public and private assets and their markets.

Examples of alternative assets are real estate, gold, private equity, hedge funds, art, wine, precious metals—lots of things. Why are alternatives advantageous? Well, let's look at real estate, for example, because it's so familiar. Yes, the real estate market is now cyclical and has been obviously so since 1999, but it is far less subject to volatility than assets traded within a secondary market. For example, the stock market lost around 10% overnight. It took real estate three years to fall 30%. In real estate, transactional friction slows down price movement, and there's no secondary market affecting the value. The value of real estate is privately negotiated and largely driven by fundamentals—even if it is traded at the margin. It's not like real estate has an arbitrary value dictated by some omnipotent invisible hand. That's an important point.

Also, citing real estate again, the income on real estate, on residential property specifically, is even less volatile. People are paying rent in a financial crisis, and they're paying rent in the economic boom. It changes some, obviously, but that change is not as dramatic. That's another consideration. The third consideration is that you can control that investment, and if you know what you're doing, that can make all the difference.

For example, instead of just buying a piece of real estate, I could say, "Well, in the previous financial crises, real estate lost 30% of its value. I can't afford to lose 30% of my money, so maybe instead of just buying, I will lend against real estate, and I will require a minimum down payment of 30%. That way, if the property loses 30%, my investment hasn't been touched, and I still have my income from it. That's one simple example. You can use options, you can use swaps, you can do all sorts of things. You can design various capital structures to accomplish various risk-adjusted return profiles. The idea is that not only is the asset not susceptible to secondary market volatility, but you can also control the way in which you invest in it.

Now, control is a double-edged sword. People irrationally believe that because they control something, it's less risky, and this is generally not true. For example, a lot of people who are afraid of flying are more than happy to jump behind the wheel of a car because they feel like they control the outcome of that mode of travel. The chance of them getting killed in a car accident is much greater than the chance of them blowing up in an airplane, but they feel like their control over the situation is a risk mitigation strategy even though it's not. Nowhere is this more obvious within the domain of investing than with real estate. You can even see this phenomenon within family offices.

A family office is a financial advisory firm that advises a single affluent family that generally has at least nine figures in assets, and it provides comprehensive financial services such as tax planning—everything—whereas your regular financial advisor just advises a bunch of less wealthy people. What's interesting is that generally speaking, this affluent family will trust a financial advisor to trade stocks and bonds and effectively manage their entire financial life, but when it comes to real estate, the family wants to do it themselves. They take a DIY approach. They don't know anything about investing in real estate, but they think it's a simple business because they can touch and feel it, they can control it, so they feel like they're going to do well, and they invariably don't. They just buy the market, and if you're going to just buy the market, you might as well buy stocks; that market does a little better.

Real estate does have some tremendous inherent advantages, but you have to know how to take advantage of them and effectively apply the sophistication of finance to real estate. It's not about just going out there and buying a property at a discount. That's what these families tend to pursue regardless of the dedicated financial services they're paying handsomely for.

So, just because you can do it yourself doesn't mean that it's less risky, but it can be if you know what you're doing. And just because gurus put out courses that allow you to "learn how to invest in real estate in a couple of weeks," doesn't mean that you're actually prepared to do it in an effective way. You can potentially lose more money and incur more risks than if you did just buy the stock market. While real estate investing has no barrier to entry in terms of required education, that should not be construed as a free pass for the uneducated guy with a high school diploma. If anything, the lack of a formal framework requires active real estate investors to take on more initiative and responsibility when it comes to their professional education than the credentialed financial advisor, and that's an incredibly important point to make that I think is lost on 99% of real estate people.

DIY REAL ESTATE

Interviewer: Where can we learn how to intelligently invest in real estate if we do want to take the DIY approach?

Ben Summers: I think Carleton Sheets's course was amazing. Now, some of it is dated, obviously, and as the economy changes, the strategies you're going to employ need to change.

Here's the problem… it lies at the crossroads of marketing and operations. People are lazy. For them to buy something, they've got to think it's simple, and the demand in the information market is for a product that gives you a five-step process to be successful. The fact of the matter is, it's not a five-step process, and it's not a single formula.

The Carleton Sheets course included a comprehensive set of tools to apply to any market condition to be successful in real estate. He even dedicated a fair amount of time to the idea of creative thinking. You have to be able to solve your own problems, but for some reason, that was just lost on people. He got a bad rep for that, but the content in that course was great. Since Carleton Sheets, many other gurus have started up real estate investing information businesses with valuable information. Bigger Pockets is an online source of free real estate investing education. Clear Real Estate Online has some pretty good, free information as well, and there are others with courses that teach one specific strategy here and one specific strategy there. They're effective in teaching their strategy, but it's not a comprehensive approach to investing.

Again, they are teaching you tools, but they're not necessarily teaching you under what circumstances you should use those tools and how those tools should be wielded in various economic environments. Even more important to consider is how to use these tools in conjunction with other investing and financial tools. Real estate investors and their gurus tend to think that real estate is the only investment, and financial advisors tend to think that stocks and bonds (and maybe REITs) are the only investments. It's important to understand all asset classes and how to work with them using the full palate of financial tools to maximize risk-adjusted performance.

Each asset class contributes different benefits and disadvantages to a portfolio. You have to understand finance in a comprehensive sense to be able to use real estate effectively, and I would say that my Accredited Investment Professional course is the only program available that provides such a comprehensive perspective. It is effectively a financial course to teach people about investing in general, bridging the gap between traditional finance and alternatives such as real estate. It covers everything from the nature of money and the various types of asset classes with the professionals and processes involved in these various markets, to how real estate fits in and how to use real estate as part of a holistic approach that maximizes what really matters: your ability to generate strong risk-adjusted investment investment performance.

Full disclosure, it's not a step-by-step recipe. By definition, it can't be because market conditions change, economies change, and you have to be able to create solutions that solve the problems that each of these unique phases of the market and circumstances creates. There's no such thing as a cookie-cutter approach, but it will teach you the tools and the fundamentals required to navigate this upside-down economic climate in the most effective way possible like a top-tier financial professional.

ALTERNATIVES TO REAL ESTATE

Interviewer: Are there any other private alternative assets that you recommend investing in other than real estate?

Ben Summers: Yes, but I advise against thinking in terms of asset class. The approach should be a search for maximum risk-adjusted performance across all asset classes to pick the best-performing assets that meet your liquidity needs, again, regardless of class.

This gets into the discussion of what is an investment and how do you choose one. A lot of people think in terms of projected returns but tend to not account for the risk in any meaningful way. Just like on a balance sheet, if you look at your assets but don't take into account your liabilities, your perception of your net worth will be skewed. You'll have an overly optimistic view of your net worth if you don't take into account your debt. If you look at an investment and its expected return but don't look at the risk that you're incurring with that investment, you're creating the same type of perception problem as what I described with the balance sheet example. You have an overly optimistic appraisal of the quality of your investments.

You have to understand what risk is, and then you have to understand how to measure it. Once you understand how to evaluate risk-adjusted performance, then you can apply these skills and techniques to evaluate any type of asset that you come across to determine how good it is relative to any other investment opportunity.

Let's take a look at real estate as an example of how making investment decisions based solely upon asset class is a meaningless approach. I'd say real estate is good, but that's too generic. You can overpay for a property, and that's a bad deal, or you can effectively steal a property acquiring it at a huge discount, and that's a great deal. Real estate as a market is not good or bad. It depends upon the individual opportunity, and you must evaluate every individual opportunity utilizing a meaningful understanding of risk-adjusted performance. You've got to measure the risk, you've got to measure the return, and then you can make a meaningful comparison. This is a valuable lesson with respect to critical thinking skills in general: forget category labels, evaluate the individual.

I really tire of hearing people respond to my advice to measure risk with, "Oh, it's too complicated." or, "That's too academic." That perspective communicates laziness and ignorance. Measuring risk, quantitative risk analysis, is simply the means of making an accurate, objective statement about the most important characteristic of investing. It's the grown-up approach to making investment decisions.

There are people in your life that you trust, and there are people in your life that you don't. How do you make the decision about who is trustworthy versus who is not? The answer is simple. The people you trust are those you've known for a long time, and over that time, they have not misled you. Past performance, past experience with these people, has demonstrated that they don't lie, and so in the future, you expect that they're not going to lie.

We look at what somebody has done in the past, and the further back you can look into the past, the more meaningful your expectations about the future become. If you met somebody yesterday and they haven't lied to you yet, you may afford them a little bit of trust, but the relationship has not existed long enough to establish a meaningful level of trust. The longer you've known someone, the more trust you'll have in them if they haven't lied to you over that period.

The idea of relying on historical data as the only meaningful indication about what might happen in the future is fundamental to philosophy: it's epistemology 101. Finance is not exempt from the fundamental laws of nature and reality.

The same approach should apply to financial assets and professionals. The longer you can look back at the historical performance across various economic climates, in particular, a minimum of a full market cycle, preferably multiple market cycles, the more complete picture you have. Whichever asset lost the least amount of value over that period is probably the safest asset to buy. The mathematics takes that analysis and translates it into a meaningful, objective, and comparable scale. Again, it's not a matter of picking an asset class from an ivory tower; it's a matter of understanding how to evaluate an individual investment opportunity, to measure its risk-adjusted performance across a minimum of one complete market cycle, and then invest in the assets available to you with the best risk-adjusted performance.

BACKTESTED RISK-ADJUSTED PERFORMANCE FOR PRIVATE EQUITY

Interviewer: I'm aware that there are firms that buy fledgling businesses, improve them, and then resell them. These private equity firms would look at the prior performance of the target company and then have to determine the cost of the turnaround and the chances of selling the business at that improved value? How do you measure the risk-adjusted performance of such a strategy?

Ben Summers: That's interesting. First and foremost, that's what my business does, which separates it from everyone else. We take operators of private businesses and then look at what their risk-adjusted performance is when you fix all the problems. The way you do that is by breaking down that target company into every possible variable that contributes to its performance, measuring each of those variables individually, and then improving the ones that can be improved.

Once you've done that, then you weight and consolidate all those variables into one aggregated set of performance data. While that's a very simple description, it takes an effort, in addition to exceptional critical thinking and mathematics skills to do well.

When we're working with our clients, they're already starting from a position of strength. They've already got some very redeeming qualities. Generally, it's access to quality deal flow—maybe great profitability across market cycles.

The first step in the process is to translate the management of the business or investment model into a comprehensive set of systematic rules, then identify every possible variable associated with those rules that contribute to performance.

Of course, there are infinitely many variables that contribute. It's impossible actually to account for every one, but you want to account for as many as you possibly can and accurately identify those that contribute the most to performance and effectively aggregate smaller variables at the same time. You'll see which dials to turn and which have the greatest impact on the profitability of the company. You can manage each of those individually and then reconsolidate those variables to get an aggregated output. Plugging data into those variables beyond the start date for the company and analyzing it is called constructing a theoretical track record and backtesting.

Even if a firm has been in operation for a long time, if we improve some aspect of their model, we've changed the way the variables are used. So that would also be a case that involves backtesting. You've changed the way they do business in a certain way, so one or more of their variables are different, and you need to take those variables and run them back across a minimum of one complete market cycle with the actual data that we've experienced over that period. You'll see the historical performance of those variables over time and their effect on the overall aggregated performance.

One simple example might be buying an airline. An important variable in managing an airline is the cost of fuel. Maybe they were buying fuel at spot price, and you could see that they had historically high volatility in fuel costs, and that was really hurting their business when fuel prices went up. An alternative to suffering that volatility is to buy forward contracts. Forwards allow you to lock in a commodity price for X period, and say, "All right, instead of buying fuel at spot, I'm going to lock in fuel at a fixed price over a specific period of time."

Next, we look at what your fuel forward contracts would have done over the past 10 years relative to what that spot price did. You can now see what your cost was for a forward-driven fuel acquisition strategy versus a spot price-driven fuel acquisition strategy and how that contributes to your P&L statement. That's one very simple example, but it's not simple. It's not for lazy people. It's not like you're going to snap your fingers and pontificate about what this company would have done. It takes a lot of research and effort and critical thinking to first identify these variables, and then determine how to backtest them. Does that make sense?

Interviewer: Yes. It's not a paint-by-numbers process. You have to understand the underlying fundamentals and be able to intelligently analyze that understanding, which I think is what a lot of this book is about. It helps you understand the necessary foundational considerations, starting with what is going on financially, both in this country and in the world in general, and then moves into more specific knowledge, albeit complex, that you can use to take control of your financial life.

Ben Summers: Yes, and that can be frustrating for a lot of people. I get that. There are certain cultures that are more inclined to accept this complexity than others. I grew up in one that had no patience for such things. A lot of people believe that if something is complex, it must be bullshit. Most people just want the simple version and believe that all complexity is contrived to hide scams. Sometimes, things are just inherently complex. For example, look at the construction business, where the barrier to entry is cost. If you want to start a construction company, you need to have a lot of money to buy equipment to get into that business. The barrier to entry into high finance and investing is not money; it's intelligence.

The nature of the business is complex. It's evolved that way, and so to ignore that complexity is to say, "I just don't care enough about money to be bothered," and that's fine, you can take that position if money's not that important to you. Some people do take the approach of, "I'm going to be a real estate investor because it's fun," or, "I like doing rehab projects on houses, and if I make some money, great." If you want to be a serious, professional investor, though, there's no way to avoid the complexity and still responsibly and ethically manage your professional obligations. It's just the nature of the beast. I wish successful investing could be boiled down to a simple paint-by-numbers approach, but it can't. I'm providing an introduction to the fundamental pillars of finance that enable you to control your positions and be successful. You can ignore the complexity, but the extent to which you do is the extent to which you are incurring risk that you don't understand. That's not wrong, but just know that the consequences can be devastating.

Interviewer: So, the smart investor looks for opportunities with a high barrier to entry that they can overcome, which keeps a lot of other people out minimizing competition?

Ben Summers: It's rarefied air. It is not an exaggeration to say that the stuff I'm talking about, the level I'm talking about, is known by fewer than one in a million people. As with anything worthwhile, it takes effort to get there—in this case, intellectual effort—and yes, effort weeds people out reducing competition.

HOW TO USE DEBT

Interviewer: In terms of financial instruments, is there a way to use debt to improve our financial position, or is all debt bad and should be avoided or removed as quickly as possible?

Ben Summers: No, not all debt is bad. We live with a debt-based fiat currency, and to ignore that, to refuse to participate as a matter of principle, is an expensive position to hold. It's the nature of our economy, so you might as well use it to your advantage. To a great extent, the macro-economy, the monetary system that we have, is like a very large wave. You can either choose to surf and navigate that wave in an elegant and effective way, or you can get yourself killed trying to run up against it. Debt can be tremendously advantageous if properly used.

A very simple and straightforward way to invest, given a certain set of needs that you might have in terms of liquidity, risk and return, is to use debt to lend to residential real estate investors in a responsible way. It's not a simple thing to do, but it's not terribly complicated either. That is an example of issuing debt to profit, analogous to what a bank does. If you borrow at one interest rate to lend at a sufficiently higher interest rate on responsible terms, that's an example of good debt.

Utilizing debt in the capital structure of any investment is a brilliant means to generate quality risk-adjusted performance. That being said, for my firm's funds, we don't actually use debt. We use unlevered, non-convertible preferred equity in lieu of debt because preferred equity can't foreclose. It looks like debt, it talks like debt, it walks like debt, it meets all of the risk-adjusted return and liquidity needs of the investor who buys it, but it minimizes risk for everybody. In the extraordinarily unlikely event of a hiccup in cash flow, a missed dividend payment can be caught up later with compounding and without causing a problem. If it's true debt and you miss a dividend payment, that could wreak all kinds of havoc around default and potential foreclose, so preferred equity can mitigate risk all around. So yes, fixed income instruments, debt or preferred equity, can be tremendously valuable tools.

Taking a step back, there are two general types of investment instruments that you can buy, and they serve two different purposes. One is for growth; the other is for income. Growth investments are generally equity, and they usually don't pay much in terms of dividends or cash flow. You hold them to grow. You might buy a company that's worth $1 million today, and hopefully, in ten years, it's worth $10 million so you can sell it a make a lot of money over that period. You only recognize the profits when you sell it, but you didn't need the profits any sooner, typically because your income came from your job or primary business. With a growth strategy, you don't need income from your investments; you need your investment portfolio to grow and get as big as it can, as fast as it can, with the least amount of risk.

However, when you're 70 years old, growth would be great, but what's way more important than growth is income. You probably don't have a job anymore, Social Security sucks, and you need your couple of million dollars in savings to give you an income every month to replace the job you retired from; you can't afford to lose money, meaning you have a very low risk tolerance. This is where fixed-income instruments come into play, and the most common example is debt. When you buy debt, probably in the form of bonds, it generally doesn't grow at all; it just pays you reliable interest payments every month. Note that I'm talking about bonds in the general sense. There are many different types of bonds: zero coupon, etc. some of which may not pay a dividend.

In summary, debt instruments are generally suited for people who need income from their investment portfolio, whereas equity or stock is what would be utilized to accommodate growth in an investment portfolio. Bonds are a form of debt. Of course, instead of just buying bonds that are subject to a secondary market, you could lend in real estate and dictate your own terms. But, with great power comes great responsibility. There's a lot to learn to understand how to do that effectively and make it truly a better risk-adjusted play than just buying a bond.

HOW TO USE PERSONAL DEBT

Interviewer: How about personal debt? Is there a way to use personal debt intelligently?

Ben Summers: There's a difference between debt and leverage. In general, simple debt is bad, but now we're getting into a vernacular issue. Leverage can be bad for the system at the extent it is currently employed, but good for you as an individual. What is leverage? Leverage is borrowed money used for the purpose of investing, which grows your asset base. Banks use it all the time. A bank will borrow money from you at some low-interest rate in a savings account or a CD. They might pay you 1% on a 1-year CD, let's say, and then they'll take that $1,000 that you put in your CD, and they'll lend it out at 9%, making an 8% spread, and that doesn't take into account the fractional reserve process that allows them to scale that initial capital ad infinitum as time deposits aren't subject to reserve requirements .

The bank incurs debt when it accepts your CD. They owe you money. They take your money, and they have to pay you back with interest, but that's good debt for them because they take that same money and use it to make more money in a very straightforward way. I'd borrow as much money as I could, every day, to accomplish that end, and that's exactly what banks do.

On the flip side, a common example of bad debt is borrowing to buy a car. Let's say you buy a $20,000 car and get a $20,000 loan on it. You own the car for three years, and your car is now worth $10,000, and you owe $15,000 on it. That's bad debt, because that car does not generate any income, nor does it grow in value—it actually loses value. It's the opposite of an investment; it saps your income and net worth. You lost $10,000 over three years, but you still owe $15,000.

In short, debt that is used to make money safely is good debt. Debt that is used for things that cost you money, things that depreciate, is bad debt. But you have to take it one step further. It's not enough to say that if you're borrowing money for something profitable, you can borrow any amount of money on any terms and be fine. At a minimum, the income should exceed the debt service on what you're borrowing.

Here's another example of bad debt that some people might think is good debt. It is generally bad debt to borrow

$100,000 to buy a $100,000 single-family residence that needs six months of rehab before you can rent it. Why? Because you have to pay interest on that debt for six months, but you don't have any income to pay that interest. It's just not there, so you're borrowing from profits that you may or may not realize. What's the probability of achieving that profit? If you're in real estate, I'd bet a lot of money that you don't know. You're incurring an unknown amount of risk.

Alternatively, like we do with our clients, if you're a value-add multifamily real estate investor and not investing in a bomb blast of a building, it's still going to generate some income. We look at the income that this property is currently generating, and then we have an expectation of what it will generate after it's stabilized, but right now, it's generating some income. One of the limits on debt is that the income that it's currently generating has to exceed the debt service on what you borrow. This relationship is referred to as a debt service coverage ratio, or DSCR. As a simple example, if this $100 million building is only generating $100,000 a year in net operating income, then we can only afford debt to the extent that the interest on that debt is $100,000 assuming it's an interest-only instrument. You also have to take into account the term of the loan versus the expected liquidation schedule of the leveraged asset, which is hugely important to align for what should be obvious reasons.

If it's an amortized instrument, then that $100,000 has to cover the principal and interest payments over that year. Again, it's not a simple black-and-white answer. There is some critical thinking involved in deciding how to use debt. When you're buying anything, how much debt should you use versus how much equity? In other words, how much should you borrow versus how big your down payment should be? There's a method to that madness, and there's an answer to that question. There is an optimum ratio of debt to equity that maximizes the risk-adjusted return of that asset. All of these things can be calculated.

Interviewer: The main reason I asked that question was that, as a consumer, we often feel like there's so much hidden from us. I was curious if there was some other reason to carry debt other than for the purpose of increasing income.

Ben Summers: There is. In general, it is a bad idea to attempt to predict the future. Mankind is inherently terrible at predicting the future. We're very good at rationalizing why things happened after the fact, but we're very bad at predicting what's going to happen. If, for example, you knew that the dollar was doomed, and you knew that we were going to experience substantial inflation over some period, and you knew what that period was, then you should borrow your ass off because to the extent that inflation exceeds the interest rate on the debt that you borrow, you're making money. Do you understand why?

Interviewer: Is it because if you're borrowing money now, what you're getting now is more valuable than what it's going to be in the future. The dollar itself is going to be less valuable.

Ben Summers: That's correct. Inflation is a tax. The government can tax you in a couple of different ways. It can say, "All right, we're going to make you pay 10% of your income every year, or 30%, or whatever. You just have to write a check for a percentage of your income to the government, and that's a tax." That hurts, and everybody is aware of this, but it's very straightforward. However, there's an alternative, more sinister way of accomplishing the same end that eludes almost everyone, and that's inflation. The definition of inflation by the Austrian economic perspective is not an increase in prices, but it's a growth in the money supply. The way the growth in the money supply affects prices is impossible to predict, it's chaotic, and it will materialize in any number of unpredictable ways over some arbitrary period of time.

Right now, we are experiencing substantial inflation in the form of the price of stocks, the equities market. That's inflation, in no uncertain terms. You won't ever hear anyone on CNBC say that, but that's what it is. Here's what I'm talking about. Let's say the tax rate is 50% because that makes the math easier, and effectively, that's what it is when you count all the tax that you pay—tolls, gas tax, cigarette tax, sales tax—there are tons of them. Let's say the tax rate is 50%, and you make $100,000 a year. The government can simply demand 50% of everybody's income, so you have to write them a check for $50,000. That's one way to do it, but taxes are painful to pay and very unpopular.

There's another way to get half of your income. The government could say, "What we're going to do is grant ourselves the authority to create money, and we're just going to print $100,000." The government doesn't make you pay any taxes, it just prints $100,000 for itself.

Now, the government has $100,000, and you have $100,000. There's now $200,000 in this little hypothetical economy. What's happened now is there's $200,000 chasing the same amount of goods and services that were previously only being chased by $100,000. Once that doubling of the money supply matriculates through the economy, what happens? It cuts your purchasing power in half. Twice as much money in an economy eventually leads to prices being twice as high, assuming no additional products or services were added. So, even though you have $100,000 in your hand, it only has the value that $50,000 had when there was only $100,000 total in the economy. Does that make sense?

Interviewer: Yes. Instead of taking half of our money, they make it worth half as much.

Ben Summers: That's right. They still, effectively, take half of your money, but instead of taking it from you directly, they simply dilute yours. Purchasing power is a much more important concept to consider than simply some amount of money without context. They take half of your purchasing power by creating money for themselves. That is exactly what inflation is. Inflation is a tax, and there is a crony relationship between the Federal Reserve and the government to supply the money that it needs. That is a tax because every dollar that's printed dilutes your purchasing power. But that's way too complicated for the average person to understand, so he doesn't really care. Inflation, who cares?

Inflation is generally officially reported to occur at a rate of 2% a year, which people mostly ignore. It's really greater than 2% a year. Here's an example: there is one thing I buy a lot of: Chipotle chicken bowls. Chipotle used to cost me $6.25 for a bowl, and now it costs me $12. That's almost a 100% increase over six years.

These 2% inflation numbers are bullshit. Real inflation is much higher, and it's a tax. The population is being cooked like the frog in the pot of water where the temperature is slowly raised until it's too late to jump out. That's exactly how inflation is managed, and it is deliberately managed in this way. It is not a conspiracy theory to suggest that the psychology of the math is taken into account in this sleight of hand.

HOW TO TAKE ADVANTAGE OF INFLATION

Interviewer: Is there a way that we can take advantage of inflation?

Ben Summers: By borrowing, but it's a dangerous game because the market is manipulated. If I invest in a bond that pays 10% and the inflation rate is 10%, at the end of the year, I've broken even.

I'll try to explain this with an example: If I have $100 now, at the end of the year, a 10% inflation rate results in that $100 only being worth $90. If I borrow $100 now at 10% interest under no inflation, spend none of it except to pay the 10% interest-only payment due at the end of the year, then I have $90 left from what I borrowed at the end of the year. Do you see how, in these two scenarios, the 10% rate of inflation and the 10% interest rate act on my money in the same way? The interest rate and inflation rate are interchangeable. If the rate at which I can borrow matches the rate of inflation and I can use that money today, it's a break-even situation.

If I can borrow money for less than the rate of inflation to buy something today assuming that thing doesn't lose value and has a price that follows the rate of inflation, that's a win. Here's why. Say the inflation rate is 10%, so again, $100 at the beginning of the year is reduced to $90 in purchasing power by the end of the year. Let's say I can borrow at 2%. I buy some asset that doesn't change in value. I borrow $100 to buy it today, but it only costs $98 today, and I borrow $100 because I know I have to pay 2% interest. I borrow $100, I buy this $98 asset today, I take my leftover $2, and I pay my 2% interest. Make sense?

At the end of the year, let's compare the two scenarios. The person who only held cash has $100 in cash that's worth $90 right now because of inflation. The person who borrowed to buy an asset can sell that asset today for over $107—the $98 purchase price increased by 10% due to inflation over that year. His net worth is over $107. You can use debt as a way to combat inflation, but you must borrow at a lower rate than inflation, and the average interest rate must always be less than the average inflation over that period. Of course, you must have the cash flow to support the debt payments.

Interviewer: How often does that happen?

Ben Summers: A lot. Here's an example. I can buy bonds that generate a 5% return, and I can borrow against those bonds at an 80% LTV for 100 basis points, one percent interest. Conservatively speaking, actual inflation right now is probably around 5 or 6%. I've got a 4% plus spread between my debt service and inflation. I can use that borrowed money to buy more bonds, or any other asset that reliably rides the rate of inflation, then borrow again against the new bonds, or whatever asset I just bought with leverage to buy even more; I can repeat this process until LTV constraints don't allow me to borrow anymore. As long as I've got a place to put that money right now that will reliably generate returns in excess of the interest rate I can borrow at, then I should borrow as much as I possibly can. The key is identifying assets that most efficiently express inflationary pressures. When you do that, you're leveraging inflation, but it's worth noting that there's more to consider than just the relationship between interest rates and inflation rates: cash flows, asset volatility, loan terms, and other important considerations must be taken into account.

But in short, you take on debt as an inflation play, the average interest rate over the loan term has to be below the inflation rate over that same period, and you have to put that money into something today that will be worth at least as much in the future when you need to liquidate, and that something should throw off enough income to cover the debt service as well. If all those criteria are met, then yes, that's a good way of using debt.

WHAT TO DO AS AN EMPLOYEE

Interviewer: For those of us with jobs, should we start taking action to switch to jobs with real productivity or is that going to make a difference when the big collapse comes? Will it make a difference if we have a job that's based on real productivity, for example, where something is manufactured?

Ben Summers: I would argue that it's never a good practice to sell yourself to a corporation as a cog that only functions within its machine. The best advice is to invest in yourself.

You should position yourself to provide independent value—value that you can take pride in and that others will recognize. There are tools that can help you monetize your value through effective marketing, but you first have to possess value to market. Regardless of what you do, I would argue that it's in everyone's best interest, not only as a means to insulate yourself from economic turmoil, but just for own your sense of self-worth and independence, to invest in your knowledge and ability to create value. I don't mean trivial knowledge or academic knowledge necessarily. It could be academic knowledge, but knowledge that is marketable, that translates into value that you and others can recognize. Ideally, your value is not sensitive to market cycles.

That's one of the reasons so many people are drawn to real estate; people tend to think in terms of the adage that everybody needs a place to live, and it's true. Of course, as we've said before, there's more to it than that, but my ability to provide capital to any quality investment business is something that is going to be needed across market cycles.

Again, in the same breath, it's important to marry this investment in your development for the purpose of creating value with your own passions and interests. You have to really care about what you are pursuing to do it well and meaningfully.

It is never good practice to chase money for the sake of money. Chase knowledge and money will come as the byproduct of that knowledge. I'm chasing knowledge about money because I recognize how important it is in the global sense. Only chasing money for personal gain is a myopic view that almost invariably leads to failure.

Are there successful people who chase money? Yes, and there are also lottery winners every week. That doesn't mean it's a prudent way forward. You have to pursue your passion, and when you pursue your passion, you will be motivated to dive into the depths of the discipline and to fulfill your maximum potential in that domain.

To have your value recognized in whatever domain you decide to pursue, at some point you're going to have to make an earnest effort to understand the psychology and the needs of the people you've decided to serve—no matter how far their psychology deviates from yours. You must give people what they value in the manner that they are able to recognize and receive it, which will often be irrational from your perspective.

HOW TO CALCULATE RISK

Interviewer: How would an investor go about determining which factors they need to consider to calculate risk? I know you offer a risk-adjusted performance calculator web application that helps people with all of this, so how do I know which numbers to enter into it?

Ben Summers: Financial risk is operationally defined as the degree to which the price of a given asset has historically moved up and down. The more it's moved, the riskier it is. If you want something with low financial risk, you find something that has very little historical price movement.

My calculator is simply an aggregate of the major risk calculations, the major risk metrics, and it analyzes the annual returns of any given single investment or portfolio of investments. The only inputs for these calculations are return numbers. This calculator is designed to work with annual return numbers because it is meant to analyze illiquid alternatives, but the same calculations are applicable to liquid assets. The only difference is that the interval of return data should correspond with the liquidity of the asset. So, for example, ideally speaking, a publicly-traded stock should be analyzed with daily return data, especially if you're day trading. In practice, though, we generally analyze hedge funds trading equities on a monthly basis, which gives us a good enough approximation, especially considering that we're looking across one or more complete market cycles.

So, when you're trying to decide what to invest in, you're looking for the highest returns that you can possibly achieve without creating a great deal of variability in those returns. You can start by simply eyeballing historical data for the assets or portfolios you're considering. Once you've narrowed down the field, it's time to start utilizing the calculations to tell you precisely how various investments compare. The risk-adjusted performance calculator makes this process easy.

You're likely to be often surprised by what the numbers tell you.

If you're an asset manager structuring a new investment strategy, the goal is to generate the highest possible returns with the least amount of movement in price. There are a lot of variables that must be evaluated in terms of structure, asset selection, valuations, trade signals, etc. Investment strategies with comparable overall performance can have incredibly different levels of complexity.

When you are trying to construct an investment strategy, you have to take into account every possible variable that contributes to your overall performance and periodic—monthly, quarterly, annual—return numbers. My ability to do that is where I earn my keep. It's a problem-solving skill, not a cookie-cutter recipe.

A simple example would be buying real estate to hold for income. You need to look at the real estate you're potentially going to buy and its historical income going as far back as possible. A one-market-cycle lookback is good, but you want to go back as far as you possibly can to evaluate the relationship between the income and the value. That ratio will tell you what's the most you should pay. Of course, there are other important variables to consider as well, such as the capital structure, terms of debt, rehab and construction risk, etc., but market risk is the place to start.

Now, today's market may dictate that a given seller won't accept what you're willing to pay, so you may have to make an effort to find what you're looking for, but that's a very simple risk management technique for determining how to buy a piece of property to hold for income. If you're not able to source sufficient deal flow with a buy and hold strategy, you may have to increase the complexity of your strategy to source deal flow that meets your risk-adjusted performance targets.

RISK IN WORDS AND NUMBERS

Interviewer: What are some examples of factors that normally don't come in the form of numbers?

Ben Summers: Almost none of the considerations most people use to make investment decisions rely on meaningful numbers. People like stories, but stories are just the starting point. A story has to be translatable into numbers; otherwise, it's useless. Investing is absolutely, unequivocally a numbers game. For you to ask me to help you manage risk in words would be no different than asking me, "What should my expected returns be, and tell me without using numbers?" The answers in-kind are, "Your returns should be high; your risk should be low." Words alone don't tell you very much.

Just as expected return is a number, risk is also a number. Investment decisions based upon quantified expected returns and risk as a story are no different than keeping your checkbook by inputting the numerical value of the deposits and using only adjectives such as "big" and "small" to account for withdrawals.

Interviewer: So, most of the factors that somebody will look at will be numerical?

Ben Summers: They have to be. The story can tell you where to look for the number. Remember the old adage: there are lies, damn lies, and statistics. That's true if the statistical data does not accurately represent the system that you're analyzing or only partially represents it. The story points you in the direction to find the numbers that you need to analyze.

Can you fail with a purely quantitative approach? Absolutely. Mathematics is just a language that has to be skillfully applied to represent reality accurately. Herein lies the difference between simple mathematics and physics.

You can be a great writer, but that doesn't mean you can produce an accurate article about a subject you're not familiar with.

Physicists know how to apply the language of math to describe systems accurately, including financial ones.

Your challenge as a professional investor is to use numbers to comprehensively and accurately represent your investment model, and if those numbers don't accurately represent your investment model or if those numbers are not comprehensive in their representation of the investment model—for example, if they don't account for fat tails and their impact—the numbers will fail you. This requires you to have both a thorough understanding of the mathematical branches of statistical mechanics and probability theory in addition to economics and finance.

Interviewer: Is everything relatively easy to put into numbers?

Ben Summers: If you're managing your own investment portfolio, it should be, but you'd be surprised by how many professional asset managers can't get the numbers together.

Every investment strategy has a unique set of variables to consider, and it's the responsibility of the investment manager to understand all of those variables to the extent possible and to protect himself from those he can't know. Nassim Taleb discusses this extensively in his book, *Antifragile*.

Here's an example of something you can know that most people ignore—again within the real estate space because it's an area that a lot of people are familiar with—that might be a little challenging: If your investment strategy involves a lot of construction, and you wanted to evaluate the risk associated with that construction accurately, you would take the contractors that you are getting proposals from and demand they provide you their historical estimates for all the similar work they've done with their actual times and costs to construct. Then you can measure the statistical relationship between their estimates and actual performance history to remove that blind spot of construction risk from your analysis. That's a level of rigor that no one goes through, but they should.

That particular tip is of great value for developers who are often dismissed by institutional allocators for the high risk associated with construction costs. When they're told their project is high risk, what they're being told is that the unknown variability in the costs and timing of their projects compounded by the unpredictability of the market doesn't represent a safe investment. If you understand the market quantitatively in addition to being able to measure your construction risk accurately, you've just conquered those objections. In other words, if you could accurately price the total risk of your business, what would that do for your ability to raise capital as a developer?

USING RISK MEASURES

Interviewer: Once you've calculated that risk, how do you go about using it in a practical way when you're evaluating an investment? Is that what the risk-adjusted calculator does?

Ben Summers: There were two primary purposes for developing the risk-adjusted performance calculator:
    The first purpose was to give alternative asset managers the ability to objectively measure how their investment business measures up against the rest of the capital markets because they generally don't have any idea. It gives them the ability

to identify objectively how good, or not, they actually are so that they can decide if they need to make changes to their strategy. And if they are good, it gives them the ability to communicate their value to passive investors in meaningful terms.

The second purpose was to provide financial advisors with the ability to measure the quality of private securities issues as compared to the public securities issues that they always sell. It is also for financial advisors to measure the performance of their portfolio compared to other financial advisors in the market. Nobody does this. Most financial advisors rely on providing ancillary services as a means to compete in the market. The risk-adjusted performance calculator gives them the ability to communicate the competitive advantage of their core business.

Those are the two primary functions the calculator was intended for. I want to move the industry from heuristics-based decision making to merit-based decision making. The important features of an investment are its risk, return, and liquidity. Considerations like asset class, which are currently taken to be one of the most important, are often misguided and distract from what's important.

Investment clubs allow the retail public to organize themselves into accredited and qualified purchaser entities that afford them access to the most exclusive and best-performing investments by circumventing the obstacles presented by typical financial advisors. That being said, top financial advisors use investment clubs to help their non-accredited clients gain access to the same top-performing alternatives their ultra-high-net-worth clients have access to.

INVESTMENT CLUB ISSUES

Interviewer: I've never heard of investment clubs being used in this way. This seems to be a great solution, but what should people be aware of?

Ben Summers: The fees are higher because you have an additional layer of administration, but what's important is the risk-adjusted performance net of fees. If the net performance is good, then the investment is good.

For example, if I have five million dollars, and I invest in a fund, the fund pays me that five million dollars back plus the returns. No problem. But when you're in an investment club, you have administrators (accounting, marketing, reporting, etc.) who need to get people into the club and make sure all the money is accounted for and divvied up correctly. People come into investment clubs at different times, they invest different amounts, returns accrue starting at different times for different individuals—there are a lot of moving parts.

The fund's just paying one big lump sum of money back to the club, but at the club level, somebody needs to figure out how much money goes where and be responsible for it. That has an expense associated with it. The club members' returns are going to be diluted a little because of those administrative expenses.

The second drawback is that it's generally democratic, which means mob rule. If the majority vote to do something, and you're in the minority, you've got to go along with the majority. That's a downside. However, the investment clubs that we help others organize are structured more like a republic and less like a democracy. This means that the rules of the structure constrain the mob. So, the operating agreements we help construct determine what the minimum risk-adjusted performance and liquidity profiles are. It aggregates like-minded people with shared appetites. This leaves less room for debate and mitigates potential issues when an actual allocation decision is up for vote. The votes largely become a reaffirmation of what everybody already agreed to by joining the club in the first place.

Of course, an investment club's mandate can be left open with many different types of asset allocation decisions being brought to vote, but unless it's a small, intimate group, I would advise against this format.

All that being said, investment clubs are an invaluable opportunity for those who are not ultra-high-net-worth individuals to access the same exceptional investment performance otherwise reserved for the top 0.1%.

WHAT INVESTMENT BANKS DO

Interviewer: What exactly do investment banks do?

Ben Summers: An investment bank creates or underwrites investments. We work with alternative asset managers who are able to generate sufficiently better risk-adjusted performance than what is otherwise available through the public capital markets. That includes real estate asset managers, hedge fund managers, private lenders—you name it, and if they can generate consistently strong performance, we'll work with them.

We provide them with the comprehensive capital solutions they need: debt and equity. First, there's an advisory phase. We make sure that their investment strategy and process maximize their potential for risk-adjusted performance. Then, we make sure that performance is marketable, meaning it's sufficiently better than what's available in the public capital markets.

If it is marketable, we securitize it, which means we develop the capital structure—how much debt, how much equity... do we utilize hybrid instruments, like preferred equity, mezzanine debt, any sort of warrants...

Once that's done, we create funds that capitalize these clients, and then we build out distribution to sell interest in those funds.

We also work with people and firms who are able to aggregate capital but may not have an investment strategy of their own. We help them create structures that allow them to compliantly raise money then provide them access to best-in-class alternative asset managers, which means they themselves become unique providers of superior risk-adjusted performance.

We particularly like working with financial advisors because they are the recognized gatekeepers of the industry for the public. They can do a lot of good if they're willing to make an effort, and we're happy to send retail business their way when they do.

WHAT FINANCIAL ADVISORS NEED TO KNOW

Interviewer: What does a financial advisor need to know about working with Adagio?

Ben Summers: Most financial advisors are salespeople first. The FINRA exams largely omit quantitative risk analysis, and the CFAs who have been exposed to it generally don't use it enough to be competent.

This means that virtually no one in financial distribution (RIAs and broker-dealers) incorporate quantitative risk analysis into their business. They just don't do it. The point I want to drive home and cannot emphasize enough—I can't be more passionate about propagating this—is that to be a responsible financial advisor requires an understanding of quantitative risk analysis.

To pursue an investment based upon an expectation of a quantitative return without having an equivalent understanding of the associated quantitative risk is no different than looking at a balance sheet and ignoring the liabilities while exclusively focusing on the assets. The ability and the willingness to incorporate accurate quantitative risk analysis into your practice is the opportunity to differentiate your practice from all the others within a flooded market.

Interviewer: Why isn't it being done? Why are financial advisors effectively ignoring risk?

Ben Summers: Because the culture of the industry has indoctrinated them to do so. You have these huge firms who are creating products for the purpose of selling and earning a commission or a spread. The entire motivation of the FINRA-governed industry is to sell those products and make commissions—RIAs are kind of an afterthought and are squeezed to the point that it's difficult for them to be economically viable and focus on anything but the marketing and sales efforts required to recruit clients. Merit-based portfolio construction is not the quickest and most efficient way to get money in the door.

To make matters worse, you have these cornerstones of the financial world—Goldman Sachs, J.P. Morgan, Morgan Stanley, Blackstone—whose salespeople have their logo on their business card, and that's the sales process. Brand recognition and legacy in the financial services industry is what people go after. They ignore merit because it's complicated. People know that Goldman is screwing them, but they keep doing business with them anyway. I guess the devil you know…

The SEC, the Securities and Exchange Commission, has delegated most of its workload to FINRA, which is a private self-regulatory organization, and it's organized by these biggest players. They've created a regulatory environment and culture that maintains the status quo, and the penalties for violating this minefield are draconian. Why would the biggest players create a merit-based regulatory environment that undermines their profitability? They wouldn't, and they haven't.

Our firm is built on the idea that there are people who actually care about the quality of service and products within the finance industry, and that's who we seek out. That's who this book is written for.

THE PURPOSE OF THIS BOOK

Interviewer: Is the purpose of the book to help the real estate investor understand why it's better to evaluate a property based on its potential net rent versus potential appreciation?

Ben Summers: That is a very important consideration for real estate investors, but this book is meant for all alternative asset managers and investors. There are tremendous opportunities across all alternative asset classes—from relatively simple real estate plays to the most sophisticated synthetic risk transfer strategies.

If anything, one of the motivations for writing this book is to dispel the widely held belief within the finance industry that risk-return is a zero-sum game, and to illustrate that sophisticated alternative asset managers can successfully fill some of the biggest holes in the markets.

If you go to your financial advisor, you're going to face an assumed truth that the greater the level of returns you pursue will necessarily correspond with an equivalently offsetting increase in the level of risk you're exposed to—that you can't escape this mythical, short tether that inversely binds risk and return.

One of the easiest to understand examples of the error in this line of thinking can be found in real estate: the income from real estate, the rental income, is relatively stable compared to the comparable sales values of real estate. Now, that varies from local market to local market, and there are a lot of variables to consider, but the general idea is true.

Financial risk is the amount, or degree, to which a price changes either up or down. This is called volatility. The more something goes up and down, the more volatile it is, and by definition, the riskier it is. That's what we're trying to measure. When you look at real estate—particularly residential real estate—you'll see that, especially since 1999, values, which are traditionally accepted to be based upon comparable sales, have been volatile. They went really high through 2007, then went low, and now they're well on their way up again. The income, however, did not experience such volatility. What that tells you is to construct an investment model in real estate based upon the income as opposed to the comparable sales value or the market-dictated cap rate. People will often respond with, "It's not realistic to be able to maintain deal flow with that approach." That may be true if your strategy is straight acquisitions, but lenders, for example, have the prerogative to set their basis in the form of LTV anywhere they want. Just think for yourself a little bit; derivatives give you all sorts of options in that regard.

All else being equal, if you can construct an investment model, regardless of your propensity for asset class, based upon the income that residential real estate generates, while discarding comparable sales-based value, then you'll find the risk is demonstrably lower than what you'll find in just about any other asset class. That is a unique opportunity, not just for real estate investors, but for financial markets as a whole.

We've covered financial markets, central banking, the supply of money and the instability of the markets. When you move from publicly-traded securities—public equities, bonds—and you start to move into private alternative assets, specifically real estate, then you're taking a first, accessible step outside of that corrupt system.

Now, when you take it one step further and start responsibly valuing these private alternative assets, such as looking at real estate from the perspective of income, you've taken one more step in minimizing the problems associated with the public markets.

As illustrated in the charts shown within this book, you see the big bubble during the preceding period and early during the financial crisis. You also see that, on a relative basis, the rental income didn't move very much.

While everybody who was invested in just about everything based upon traditional valuation methods, whether it's real-time stock trading or comparable sales values in real estate, all of those people got hammered by conforming to the cultural norms. Those who had the wherewithal to recognize the stability of the income itself insulated themselves from that risk. You'll also see that the income is significant, especially when compared to its volatility.

So, you have a positive return with very little movement, very little risk, and a relatively basic example of risk and return decoupling.

CREATING MONETIZABLE VALUE

Interviewer: Is there anything you'd like to add?

Ben Summers: As I mentioned earlier, develop yourself to be as valuable as possible—to become as knowledgeable and skillful as possible in whatever fuels your passion. The effort will require blood, sweat, and tears that the overwhelming majority of people would never consider sacrificing. The vast majority of people won't recognize your efforts or your value; they will come to you with lazy, stupid, and irrational obstacles to your attempts to genuinely help them—some will even respond to your earnest efforts to help them by trying to hurt you. You're not going to like these people; you're not going to respect them; they're not going to think like you; they won't make the efforts that you make, and you'll probably view them as psychologically defective in some substantial way. But for you to convert your intrinsic value into monetizable value, you have to find a way to motivate yourself to care about them and to meet them where they are with the patience to work through whatever unfair and unreasonable difficulties they may throw at you. For me, and you can call it a psychological trick if you'd like, my drive to affect the greater good requires me to deliver value to as many people as possible—even if I may not view many of those individuals as worth the effort. Finding a way to genuinely care about others—even those you don't like—is the last bridge to cross to evolve your intrinsic value into monetizable value, and monetizable value is necessary to affect any sort of meaningful change in the world.

About The Author

Benjamin D. Summers

Ben is the founder and managing director of Adagio Group. Through the application of his extensive knowledge in quantitative finance, the application of risk engineering principles, and private securities transactions, Ben has led Adagio from a single entity real estate investment company in 2005 to become an innovative financial institution. He also has substantial senior management experience within the global energy services sector.

Ben's transition into energy and finance was preceded by a professional baseball career that began with the San Diego Padres organization. He graduated from Louisiana State University with a bachelor's of science degree in physics having studied music as a second discipline. Ben currently holds the FINRA Series 65 and Florida Real Estate Licenses.

Schedule a complimentary strategy session to discover the appropriate shadow banker's solution for you at www.adagioinstitute.org/schedule.